ACCESS TO HOUSING

Homelessness and vulnerability in Europe

Bill Edgar, Joe Doherty and Henk Meert

FEANTSA

First published in Great Britain in October 2002 by

The Policy Press
University of Bristol
34 Tyndall's Park Road
Bristol BS8 1PY
UK

Tel +44 (0)117 954 6800
Fax +44 (0)117 973 7308
E-mail tpp-info@bristol.ac.uk
www.policypress.org.uk

ISBN 1 86134 482 1

Bill Edgar is a Senior Lecturer in the Department of Town and Regional Planning, University of Dundee. **Joe Doherty** is a Senior lecturer in the School of Geography and Geosciences, University of St Andrews. They are also Co-ordinators of Research for the European Observatory on Homelessness and Directors of the Joint Centre for Scottish Housing Research. **Henk Meert** is a Post-doctoral Fellow of the Flemish Fund for Scientific Research FWO and Associate Professor in Human Geography at the Catholic University of Leuven.

The research was commissioned by FEANTSA with the financial support of the Directorate-General for Employment and Social Affairs of the European Commission. The contents of this book are partly based on research carried out by the 15 national correspondents of the European Observatory on Homelessness, with the support of their universities and research institutes in the member states of the European Union.

Cover design by Qube Design Associates, Bristol.
Printed in Great Britain by Bell & Bain Ltd, Glasgow.

Contents

Foreword

This report is another in a series of impressive research reports produced by the European Observatory on Homelessness. This report addresses an issue that is central to the macro-social fabric of homelessness: the access of the most vulnerable people to the housing market. Starting from an elaboration of the principle of social cohesion, it argues for the right to housing on the legal basis of existing international conventions and resolutions: all citizens, including the homeless and poorly housed, should have access to adequate housing at a price they can afford. The authors examine a wide range of factors working against the realisation of the right to housing through a coherent theoretical framework, which puts the complex interaction of the market, the state and civil society at the centre of their analysis. Against the background of accelerating globalisation, they vividly describe the devastating effects of one of the last ideologies of the 20th century: neoliberalism. The wealth of data in the report proves that social integration is declining at the cost of social solidarity at the beginning of the 21st century. The new imbalances in the role of the market, the state and civil society explain why the modes of 'production of homelessness' have changed in the last decade.

The declining provision of social housing, increasing cost of housing for the poor, higher eviction rates, the formation of new and covert forms of substandard housing, and growing spatial and regional segregation within and between the member states of the European Union are only the most significant among the many findings of this report. The report shows that state intervention in the area of housing has widely failed to find a coherent and effective response to the demographic, institutional and economic changes that go together with globalisation. Civil society – specifically through its main actors, the NGOs – has responded to this development by a wide variety of new approaches such as supported housing, preventive schemes and community action but cannot compensate for this overall development.

It is now widely accepted that homeless people need to be rehoused if they are to climb out of cycles of despair, street-living and indecent living conditions. Policy makers and social services providers are still looking for the most effective ways of rehousing. Housing policies are in review across Europe and this report elaborates in detail what changes – in the housing markets and in their governance – have taken place within the last decade.

This analysis is all the more important as its results fit perfectly into the new European Social Agenda to combat poverty and social exclusion based on Articles 136 and 137 of the Amsterdam Treaty, enacted following the European Council Meetings in Lisbon and Nice in 2000. It does so by showing the merits of a broad range of innovative counter-strategies, which intelligently combine market, state and civil society's actors' capacities for integrated approaches to overcome housing exclusion and prevent, alleviate or resettle homelessness. For me, the most evident conclusion of the report is that only a new social contract rebalancing markets, state intervention and the rich resources of civil society under the heading of social solidarity will be able to confront the dark side of globalisation: growing poverty, housing exclusion and homelessness.

This report is a rich resource for policy makers, managers of social services as well as housing agencies, and those interested in the plight of the homeless. I hope it will find a wide audience among decision-makers in order to overcome the burden of homelessness.

My thanks go to all the national correspondents of the European Observatory on Homelessness for their contributions to this report, and to the authors of this report Bill Edgar, Joe Doherty and Henk Meert, as well as to the staff of the FEANTSA office in Brussels.

Thomas Sprecht-Kittler
President of FEANTSA

Acknowledgements

As with previous publications in this series, our primary debt is to the 15 national correspondents of the European Observatory on Homelessness. Their national reports provided much of the raw material for this book, and their contributions at several Observatory meetings were instrumental in clarifying many of the conceptual and organisational constructs. The correspondents and their contact addresses are listed in the next section.

We would also like to acknowledge the key roles played by the members of the FEANTSA Secretariat in coordinating the project and in organising the meetings of the Observatory. Finally we would like to express our thanks to the staff at The Policy Press for their forbearance and unfailing good humour in bringing this publication to fruition.

FEANTSA and the European Observatory on Homelessness

FEANTSA (the European Federation of National Organisations Working with the Homeless) is a European non-governmental organisation founded in 1989. FEANTSA currently has a total of 74 member organisations in the 15 member states of the European Union and other European countries. FEANTSA is the only major European non-governmental organisation which deals exclusively with homelessness. FEANTSA works to facilitate networking, exchanges of experiences and best practices, research and advocacy in the field of homelessness at the European level. FEANTSA maintains regular dialogue with the institutions of the European Union and with national governments in order to promote effective action in the fight against homelessness. FEANTSA receives financial support from the European Commission for carrying out a comprehensive work programme. FEANTSA has very close relations with the institutions of the European Union, in particular the European Commission and the European Parliament, and has consultative status with the Council of Europe and with the Economic and Social Council (ECOSOC) of the United Nations.

The *European Observatory on Homelessness* was set up by FEANTSA in 1991 to conduct research into homelessness in Europe. It is composed of a network of 15 national correspondents from all member states of the European Union, who are widely recognised as experts in the field of homelessness. Each year the correspondents produce a national report on a specific research theme related to homelessness. The coordinators of the Observatory then analyse those national reports and integrate them into a European research report which focuses on transnational trends.

Contact address: FEANTSA, 194 Chaussée du Louvain 1210 Brussels, Belgium; Tel 32 2 538 66 69, Fax 32 2 539 41 74, e-mail office@feantsa.org, website www.feantsa.org

Coordinators and national correspondents of the European Observatory on Homelessness: 2000-2001

Coordinators

Bill Edgar, Co-Director of the Joint Centre for Scottish Housing Research (JCSHR), School of Town and Regional Planning, University of Dundee, Perth Road, Dundee DD1 4HT, UK; tel +44 (0) 1382 345238, fax +44 (0) 1382 204 234, e-mail w.m.edgar@dundee.ac.uk

Joe Doherty, Co-Director of the Joint Centre for Scottish Housing Research (JCSHR), School of Geography and Geosciences, University of St Andrews, St Andrews, Fife KY16 9AL, UK; tel +44 (0) 1334 463911, fax +44 (0) 1334 46 39 49, e-mail jd@st-andrews.ac.uk

Henk Meert, Research Associate of the Joint Centre for Scottish Housing Research (JCSHR), Post-doctoral Fellow of FWO Flanders, Associate Professor at the Institute for Social and Economic Geography of the Catholic University of Leuven, S. De Croylaan 42, B-3001 Leuven, Belgium; Tel +32 (0) 16 32 24 33, Fax +32 (0) 16 32 29 80, email henk.meert@geo.kuleuven.ac.be

National correspondents

Austria: Dr Heinz Schoibl, Helix Research and Consulting
heinz.schoibl@helixaustria.com

Belgium: Mr Pascal De Decker Antwerp University
pascal.dedecker@ua.ac.be

Denmark: Ms Inger Koch-Nielsen, Social Forsknings Institutet
ikn@sfi.dk

Finland: Ms Sirkka-Liisa Kärkkäinen, Stakes
sirkka-liisa.karkkainen@stakes.fi

France: Mme Elisabeth Maurel, GREFOSS-IEP, Sciences-Po, Grenoble
elisabeth.maurel@iep.upmf-grenoble.fr

Germany: Mr Volker, Busch-Geertsema, GISS e.v.
giss-bremen@t-online.de

Greece: Mr Aristidis Sapounakis, KIVOTOS
arsapkiv@mail.hol.gr

Ireland: Mr Eoin O'Sullivan, Department of Social Studies,
Trinity College Dublin
tosullvn@tcd.ie

Italy: Mr Antonio Tosi, DIAP, Politecnico di Milano
antonio.tosi@polimi.it

Luxembourg: Mme Monique Pels, Centre d'Etudes de Populations, de
Pauvreté et de Politiques Socio-Economiques
monique.pels@ceps.lu

Netherlands: Dr Henk de Feijter, University of Amsterdam
H.J.Feijter@frw.uva.nl

Portugal: Mr Alfredo Bruto da Costa, Universidad Católica Portuguesa
alfredo.bc@mail.telpac.pt

Spain: Mr Pedro José Cabrera Cabrera, Universidad Pontifica Comillas 3
pcabrera@tsocial.upco.es

Sweden: Ms Ingrid Sahlin, Department of Sociology, Gotenburg University
Ingrid.Sahlin@sociology.gu.se

United Kingdom: Dr Isobel Anderson, Housing Policy and Practice Unit,
University of Stirling
isobel.anderson@stir.ac.uk

ONE

Introduction

Recent estimates indicate that in the EU, 377 million people occupy 171 million housing units. Of these, 85% are classed as principal residences, 8% as second homes, and 7% as vacant units. Across individual member states, there are on average between 300 and 500 dwellings per 1,000 inhabitants, one dwelling for every two people in the best situations and for every three to four people in the worst. While circumstances do of course vary from place to place and from time to time, with some regions and metropolitan areas experiencing shortages and others experiencing a surplus, these figures suggest that there is no overall, absolute housing shortage in the EU. Yet aggregate estimates also tell us that three million people are presently homeless in the EU. A further 18 million are housed in inadequate accommodation, that is, in housing which lacks basic amenities, is structurally unsound, overcrowded, or does not offer security of tenure (EU Working Group Report, 2000, p 25)[1]. This book contributes to an understanding of this situation in an examination of the way in which the European housing market – both in its private and state spheres – embraces some households and rejects others, producing and reproducing conditions of housing vulnerability for significant sections of Europe's population.

Vulnerability is an inherent characteristic of homelessness and of street sleeping. It is also a characteristic of those who, driven to the margins of the private market and of state provision, are forced to occupy, for want of alternatives, relatively high-cost and inadequate accommodation. And it characterises those who, unable to find adequate accommodation through the state or in the market place, look to civil society – to the good will of friends and relatives and to charitable shelters and hostels. A further dimension of this book is the way in which civil society is imbricated in the market/state nexus and the role it plays in providing the locus of coping strategies for those unable to access housing through state or market channels.

All EU member states have in place a range of policies designed to ease access to housing for vulnerable and disadvantaged groups. These range from interventions in the private housing market in the form of property subsidies and grants, in the regulation of prices and rents, and through the provision of alternative housing. Each member state has its own story in this respect, reflecting different histories and cultures, and particular conjunctures of economic, social and political processes. Fragments of these stories will be related in the following chapters, but the focus of this book, while being sensitive to the specifics of individual nations, is on identifying European-wide trends and developments, in drawing out the common themes that traverse individual nations. In this respect four themes dominate this book: first, the expansion of an increasingly unregulated private market; second, the contraction of the state sector; third, the (re-)emergence of voluntary organisations and fourth, the role of vulnerable people themselves.

The policy context

Social cohesion and the fight against social exclusion are key issues for the EU. Access to adequate, secure and affordable housing is fundamental to the achievement of a socially cohesive and inclusive society. During the latter half of the 1990s, there has been an observable trend in all EU member states towards the withdrawal and reduction of state intervention in the housing market, particularly in relation to regulation and enforcement. The emphasis on market-led development has been associated with an increased role for private financial institutions in the supply of housing, while traditional social housing providers are coming under threat, or are being restructured on the basis of a market model. These changes, which have led to the rising cost of housing and a consequent lack of affordable housing, are liable to increase the number of households susceptible to housing distress and to increase the inequalities of housing outcomes between higher and lower income groups. These changes, therefore, contribute to the difficulties for vulnerable groups in accessing adequate housing. Understanding these changes in the housing market is critical to our understanding of the nature and extent of homelessness.

Since the early 1990s, the EU has increasingly taken an interest in two key areas of social policy: (i) combating social exclusion and (ii) promoting the modernisation of social protection systems. In relation to the first of these, the 1999 Treaty of Amsterdam reaffirms the joint competence of the EU and the member states in the field of social policy and provides a legal basis for the European Community's involvement in the fight against social exclusion. The objectives of the EU's social policies are based on the Social Policy Agreement which, through the Treaty of Amsterdam, has been incorporated into the social chapter of the 1992 EU Treaty. The objectives of this agreement, which include improving living conditions, have now been strengthened to encompass combating social exclusion as articulated in Article 136 of the Treaty of Amsterdam.

The Treaty of Amsterdam included the fight against exclusion in the provisions relating to the EU's social policy (Articles 136 and 137). Within this framework, the European Councils in Lisbon and Feira identified the fight against poverty and social exclusion as central elements in the modernisation of the European social model. At the European Council in Nice in December 2000, all member states agreed to work within the framework of four objectives:

- to facilitate participation in employment and access by all to resources, rights, goods and services;
- to prevent the risks of exclusion;

- to help the most vulnerable;
- to mobilise all relevant bodies.

Within this framework they committed themselves to prioritise the development of policies to tackle poverty and social exclusion.

These objectives relate directly to prevention of homelessness by removing barriers to access to housing. Under the first objective the member states agreed to "implement policies which aim to provide access for all to decent and sanitary housing". Under the second objective, the aim is to "put in place policies which seek to prevent life crises which can lead to situations of social exclusion, such as indebtedness ... and becoming homeless". Under the third objective, member states committed themselves to help those "facing persistent poverty ... because they have a disability or belong to a group experiencing particular integration problems" (Articles 136/7) – the latter group includes many homeless people. These objectives guided the development of the first National Action Plans for Social Inclusion (NAPs/incl) submitted in June 2001.

The European Commission communication document (EC, 2001), which summarises the first NAPs/incl, identifies eight core challenges, one of which is to ensure access to good quality, affordable housing and the development of "appropriate integrated responses both to prevent and address homelessness" (p 20). Although housing markets differ greatly across Europe, the NAPs/incl suggest that the market is performing badly (and increasingly so) in most member states in meeting the needs of low-income sections of the population[2]. To counter this, a number of specific policy measures have been identified: an increase in the supply of affordable housing and accommodation, the regulation of the lower end of the housing market, and protection for vulnerable consumers.

To the extent that the NAPs/incl are designed to tackle aspects of housing for vulnerable groups, they represent a major advance over previous European social policy initiatives. However, this programme ignores two key aspects of the problem of access to housing faced by those most at risk of exclusion. First, even where an adequate supply of housing can be maintained, housing tenure structures can act to exclude some groups through the lettings practices of both public and private sector landlords. Second, many people require support in order to sustain a tenancy. Therefore, access to housing can be difficult if appropriate support is unavailable or unaffordable.

European housing markets

Housing market changes during the 1990s have given rise to several issues of concern. For example, nearly all EU member states have recorded a growth in the level of homelessness. Throughout Europe a worrying concentration of economically and socially disadvantaged groups in older, overcrowded and low-amenity inner-city housing and in postwar social housing estates has been observed, raising concerns about the causes and consequences for social exclusion (MacLennan et al, 1996). These developments have taken place in the context of increasingly unstable national housing markets, especially in the latter half of the 1990s. The reasons for such instability have been extensively debated (Priemus et al, 1993; Ball and Grilli, 1997; MacLennan and Stephens, 1997; Kleinman et al, 1998). One of the key aspects identified is, in a major reversal of previous policy trends, the emergence throughout Europe of governmental policy preferences for private, weakly regulated market frameworks.

The emphasis on market-based reforms has been associated (according to Ball and Harloe, 1998) with an increased penetration of housing structures by institutions from the wider economy, partly as a result of financial deregulation. Financial deregulation has affected the costs of borrowing and has led to an increasing role for private money markets as government supply-side subsidies to housing investment have been reduced. This significant shift in housing finance has impacted extensively on the costs of both housing consumption and housing provision. Moreover, deregulation has often been associated with policy changes in the reform of housing subsidy and housing allowances, reforms which have been broadly driven by the need to reduce and re-target government spending. The combined effects of these changes in the nature of housing supply, housing finance and housing subsidies has been disproportionately felt by those people who are the most vulnerable to social exclusion as a result of their marginalisation in the labour market.

Furthermore, in the late 1990s specialist housing institutions were reshaped on a market model. Reforms in the governance of the housing market have changed the role of public sector and municipal authorities in housing provision, especially for low-income groups. In some countries they have also changed the orientation of non-profit housing associations towards market-based structures of operation in both housing provision and management. Additionally, shifts towards financial deregulation coupled with legislative and policy changes have affected the role of the private rented sector. The tenure structure of the housing market in many countries in Europe has changed dramatically over the last 20 years primarily reflected in the growth of home ownership and the decline in private renting (see Chapters Three and Four for discussion). However the impact of these changes on vulnerable and disadvantaged households is more marked in some countries than in others. This, in part, reflects the influence of different housing histories and cultures across individual countries. However, a key tenure split, apparent in all countries, in the context of accessibility to the housing market for vulnerable groups, is that between owning and renting (see Table 1.1).

Countries with above-average EU owner-occupation range from those associated with Mediterranean welfare regimes (Spain, Italy, Greece and Portugal), with the Atlantic/liberal regime (UK and Ireland) and with the Continental regime (Luxembourg and Belgium). In contrast, countries with a high percentage of rented accommodation (private and social) are associated exclusively with the Nordic regime (Sweden and Denmark) or the Continental regime (the Netherlands, France, Germany and Austria). Finland is exceptional in that the percentage of dwellings in each of the two major tenure groups fall

Table 1.1: Tenure structure in the EU (%)

	Owning	Total renting	Private renting	Social renting	Coop	Other tenures	Dwellings (millions)
Spain	84	15	15				19.2
Ireland	79	21	11	10			1.3
Italy	77	23	23			1	25.03
Greece	70	26	26				4.6
UK	68	32	11	21	0		24.6
Luxembourg	67	33	31	2			0.15
Belgium	67	33	28	5			3.75
Portugal	65	32	28	4			4.74
Finland	60	30	15		15	9	2.45
Austria	60	45	22	23	0		3.67
Netherlands	53	47	9	38			6.5
Denmark	53	44	18	19	7	3	2.48
France	53	39	21	18		7	28.69
Sweden	41	59	21	21	17		4.27
Germany	40	60	45	15			37.5
EU average	62	37	23	11	3	1	168.93

Sources: European Housing Statistics (2001); Ball (2002)

below the EU average. However, if co-ownership housing (a distinctive tenure in Finland) is classified as owner-occupied, then Finland emerges with a tenure structure which has more in common with countries such as the UK and Belgium than with other Nordic states. Within the rented sector the bifurcation of policy in relation to social rented and private rented housing creates a segmentation of the housing market which limits access and constrains choice particularly for those households on lower incomes or with support needs.

Social objectives in housing have been met by the provision of social housing in northern countries (Sweden, Denmark, Austria, Germany, France, the Netherlands and the UK). In these countries about a fifth of the housing stock is social rented (although this reaches 35-40% in Sweden and the Netherlands). In other countries social objectives have been pursued through market enhancing mechanisms and thus the social housing sector is small (10% or less in Belgium, Spain, Portugal and Italy) or non-existent (in Greece). A more tenure neutral view of how to pursue social housing objectives is evident in the structure of the social housing sector and the raft of policies to support low-income home-owners in Germany and Finland. While the configuration of tenures varies from region to region, housing tenure provides a clear contour of social exclusion in Europe.

Housing vulnerability, exclusion and homelessness

These changes in the housing market and the consequences they have for disadvantaged and vulnerable groups are compounded by demographic and socio-economic changes which are well documented in previous reports of the European Federation of National Organisations working with the Homeless (FEANTSA) and other research (Edgar et al, 1999, 2000, 2001). Economic changes have had a perverse effect. General economic growth across the EU often masks the growing inequality between those who can afford escalating housing costs (which are rising faster than wages) and those who, as a result of economic marginalisation, are increasingly unable to meet those costs. Globalisation and economic restructuring have contributed to the growth in low-paid and part-time employment, leaving many households with insecure incomes or reliant on housing allowances (which, in many countries, are being reviewed in the context of budget restraint). In this context it can also be observed that demographic changes which lead to an increase in the number of single-person and single-income households (which includes a growing number of female-headed households) leave an increasing number of households vulnerable to rising costs of housing and the risk of homelessness.

It is in this context that the adoption of common objectives in the fight against poverty and social exclusion at the European Council in Nice, and the explicit inclusion of access to decent housing and the prevention of homelessness, marks a significant shift in homelessness policy perspectives and approaches to addressing the problem. This shift places emphasis on the structural and institutional causes of homelessness rather than on individual pathological explantions. Furthermore, it arguably implies the 'mainstreaming' of policy responses to the problem, recognising the need for an integrated response rather than the provision of specialist services. It also stresses the need for preventative approaches rather than emergency or curative responses.

However, this policy discourse is still conducted within a rhetoric which perceives homelessness as a problem that can be solved within a defined time period, given adequate resources and appropriate targeted policies. This is to ignore the dynamics of the processes by which vulnerability in the housing market occurs and the persistence of structural inequalities which recreate the conditions of vulnerability. It also ignores the long-term nature of intervention for those who require support in order to live independently in the community. It is important, therefore, that the nature of vulnerability in the housing market is understood not just in terms of the structural, institutional, relationship and personal factors which may cause homelessness, but also in terms of the pathways into and routes out of homelessness within an understanding of the individual life course.

Responding to some of these concerns, the policy discourse within which the NAPs/incl are framed aims to prevent the risks of housing exclusion by facilitating access to necessary resources, rights, goods and services. Social inclusion and cohesion requires the recognition and the institution of social rights, social protection, social support and the provision of affordable housing for all. The effective implementation of this policy framework in relation to homelessness requires the acceptance of a broad definition of the nature of housing vulnerability and the recognition of an interrelated need for housing *and* support to prevent homelessness and to reintegrate homeless people. In this context the operational definition of homelessness adopted by FEANTSA provides a comprehensive and robust definition of housing vulnerability: housing vulnerability includes rooflessness, houselessness, living in insecure accommodation and living in inadequate accommodation.

Rooflessness (rough sleeping) is the most visible form of homelessness. People with chaotic lifestyles or unsettled ways of living may be disproportionately represented among the roofless population. Successful resettlement for rough sleepers may be contingent as much on the availability of appropriate support as on the availability of temporary and permanent housing. Houselessness refers to situations where, despite access to emergency shelter or long-term institutions, individuals may still be classed as homeless due to a lack of appropriate support aimed at facilitating social reintegration. People who are forced to live in institutions because there is inadequate accommodation (with support) in the community to meet their needs are therefore regarded as homeless. In this context, homelessness refers as much to the lack of housing as it does to the lack of social networks. Living in insecure housing (insecure tenure or temporary accommodation) may be a consequence of the inaccessibility of permanent housing. It may equally reflect the need for support to enable people to successfully hold a tenancy. The provision of appropriate support can be critical in helping people into permanent housing under their own tenancy. This classification also includes people who are involuntarily sharing in unreasonable circumstances and people whose security is threatened by violence or threats of violence (for example, women at risk of domestic abuse, racial violence or harassment). People living in inadequate accommodation includes people whose accommodation is unfit for habitation or is overcrowded (based on national or statutory standards) as well as those whose accommodation is a caravan or boat.

The concept of housing vulnerability employed in this book explicitly incorporates those households who experience homelessness as defined by the above categories. It also embraces those households, which as a consequence of life course events or inherited social characteristics, find themselves on the margins of the housing market and at risk of homelessness. In this category of vulnerability we include households which because of race, gender or sexual orientation, experience discrimination and marginalisation and households which, through periodic or long-term unemployment, family break up or illness, find it difficult to access affordable and adequate housing. Housing vulnerability applies to those who experience homelessness and to those at risk of homelessness[3]. Housing vulnerability is a condition of those who are denied access to adequate housing through the established channels of provision (the market and the state). It is an inherent condition of homelessness and it also characterises those who are driven to the margins of the private market and of social housing and forced to occupy, for want of alternatives, relatively high-cost and inadequate accommodation. It is also a condition of those who fall through the market/state nexus and are obliged to look for accommodation outwith the established channels, in civil society among friends and relatives, in informal shelters, and in charitable hostels.

Comparative themes

In attempting to develop a comparative perspective on the relationship between vulnerability and access to housing, three organisational concepts permeate this book: the concept of housing regimes, the notion of spheres of economic and social integration, and the concept of 'structuring'.

Housing regimes

In a previous book in this series (Edgar et al, 1999) we discussed the link between Esping-Andersen's (1990) welfare regime typology, typologies of social exclusion (Silver, 1994) and attempts to construct housing regimes (Daly, 1999). While it showed some correlation between housing policies and welfare policies, our review demonstrated the difficulties of describing a satisfactory typology of countries in relation to housing policies. One can not easily read, for instance, across from the four European social welfare models to models of housing policy and find a congruent match. The reasons for this lack of congruence reflect the 'schizophrenic' structure of housing in Europe – part private market, part state. Housing, as Törgersen (1987) observed, has always been the 'wobbly pillar' of the welfare state, its operation in part adhering to the laissez-faire diktats of the market, in part following redistributive precepts of the welfare state. The difficulty which Daly (1999) had in developing an adequate typology of housing regimes reflects the fact that the key variables we would choose to construct such a typology are, in themselves, difficult to define consistently across all 15 member states. The meaning of housing tenure is not the same in all countries or in the putative groupings derived from Esping-Andersen's welfare regimes. Equally, the differences in the nature of housing subsidies (either supply or consumption subsidy) make this variable difficult to measure consistently and the measurement of housing quality is also open to diverse interpretation. Nevertheless, the concept of housing regime provides a broad basis for grouping countries and has some significance for our understanding of the constraints on access to adequate and affordable housing for vulnerable groups. It is used in this book as a simple referencing framework within which to examine the diversity extant between the 15 member states.

Spheres of integration

The organisational framework that underpins this study is derived from the early work of Karl Polanyi (1944). This work makes use of the concept of 'spheres of economic integration', and distinguishes three principal spheres: market exchange, redistribution and reciprocity. Each of these spheres identifies a distinct set of social relations whereby households are integrated in the economic system and through which they gain access to economic resources required for sustenance and reproduction. While the three spheres clearly overlap and interweave in modern society, considered individually they provide a useful heuristic device whereby the complexities of the housing market and the interrelations between housing and the wider society can be explored.

Market exchange corresponds to all remunerated activities, that is, those which use money as the exchange mechanism. Simply put, in the sphere of market exchange all individuals and households develop a 'social utility', implying that they must produce goods and or services which are required by others and are therefore marketable. The most marketable product for the majority of individuals and households is labour power. The selling of their labour in the marketplace provides them with an income that allows them to rent or purchase accommodation as well as other necessities of life. The operation of the market is characterised, however, by risk, producing losers as well as winners. The most successful households in the labour market will be rewarded with a regular and decent income. Unsuccessful households are those who are employed in temporary or badly paid jobs, or are excluded entirely from both the formal and informal labour markets. To counteract these perverse aspects of market exchange, since the Second World War, social security systems have emerged in most European countries the strength and form of which varies from country to country (Esping-Andersen, 1990). These systems rely on redistribution and require that all citizens contribute to a common stock of resources, which are then redistributed according to agreed rules. Redistribution implies centralised collection and a hierarchical organisation. The slow but steady development of welfare systems from the end of the 19th century in most western countries, followed by their accelerated development since 1945, has created redistributive systems controlled by individual states and sustained by taxes and social security contributions. In relation to housing, redistribution includes subsidies to encourage home ownership as well as the provision of social housing stock.

Alongside exchange and redistribution, reciprocity provides a third sphere of economic integration. From the perspective of the individual reciprocity implies membership of social networks with symmetrical links between members and the capacity of each participant to produce useful resources. In relation to housing, the capacity to carry out repair work or the possibility of providing accommodation for a homeless relative or friend are two examples of the type of reciprocal resources which characterise these networks. Reciprocity then requires that each contribution to the social network be reciprocated – although not necessarily at the same time – by other members generally in the form of goods or services. These features of reciprocity involve mutual trust between members and a lasting commitment to the networks. The most obvious networks working in the sphere of reciprocity are extended families, ethnic communities and other small-scale networks.

In the following chapters, these three spheres of economic integration serve as an organisational and analytical framework through which we attempt to illuminate the coping strategies that vulnerable households employ to access housing. This framework allows a focus at both the micro (the behaviour of individual households) and macro (the operation of those societal structures which impact on the social production of homelessness) levels of analysis. Chapter Three deals with the growing importance of market principles in determining access to housing, while Chapter Four focuses on the restructuring of state intervention (redistribution). Chapter Five examines the nature of the macro-social trends affecting the sphere of reciprocity, and illustrates how social networks operate in this sphere in securing housing for vulnerable groups.

Structure and agency

In fashioning an understanding of the relationship between vulnerability and access to housing, the interrelating roles of 'structures' and 'agents' need to be acknowledged. Structures, given and inherited from the past, define the context, but not in a deterministic way. Structures are created by agents and, as the shifting configuration of the European housing market demonstrates, can be – and often are – changed by these same agents. The decisive agents in the context of this study – and as implied in the concept of spheres of economic integration – are those of the market (developers, property owners and financial agencies), of the state (central and local government) and of civil society (non-governmental organisations [NGOs] and voluntary and charitable organisations). This process of structuring (the symbiotic relationship between structures and agents; see Giddens, 1979, 1984) informs the analysis of the following chapters.

The adoption of a structuring perspective also implies that due recognition is given to the 'agency' role of those who experience housing vulnerability. Homeless and disadvantaged people are the victims, certainly, of the inadequacies and failings in the structures of the housing market and, not infrequently, suffer as a consequence of agency decisions. But they are not passive victims. Their proactive role and potential in coping with the condition and experience of housing vulnerability needs to be recognised and understood.

Of course the involvement of vulnerable people in active engagement with their own predicament is not new. Homeless people – deprived of adequate welfare support – have frequently demonstrated considerable innovative capacity in coping with their condition of existence. Some recent policy initiatives have sought to build on this capacity, to cultivate the participation of vulnerable people in seeking solutions to their predicament. The emergence of what has become know as 'participatory welfare' (Donzelot, 1991) has been stimulated by two conflicting tendencies. First, an ideology of individualism that requires acceptance of responsibility in return for access to services and, second, debates over the nature of control and discipline. The two are conflicting because the former is based on the drawing up of a contract – imposed and rarely negotiated – between homeless individuals and service providers. Through this contract homeless people become responsible for their own 'normalisation', their integration into mainstream society. They conform by learning the disciplines of time management and financial prudence and the principles of acceptable interpersonal and social behaviour. The latter, in contrast, is based on a view of societal structures and processes as power structures and processes, oppressing and 'colonising' individuals (see Foucault, 1979). Therefore, homeless peoples' lives are colonised in the sense that, as a condition of service provision, they are forced into conformity and compliance with the norms of the wider society. Foucault's (1979) complex view of power and power relations embraces the notion of 'resistance' on the part of the individuals and groups involved. Participatory welfare for homeless people, in the sense that it implies user involvement in the design and operation of services, creates the conditions for resistance in which the notions of normalisation and reintegration can, potentially, be challenged and reformulated.

Access to housing[4]

Access to housing, therefore, is a complex process involving – inter alia – regulation of the market, housing provision, the provision of social protection and social services support, and the empowerment of vulnerable people. These elements form the basis of this book.

A key principle of social cohesion is that all citizens should have access to adequate housing at a price they can afford. This principle falls short of guaranteeing the right to housing. However the distinction between access to housing and the right to housing is an important one which influences the approach adopted in this volume and is considered in detail in Chapter Two. Nevertheless, the objective enshrined in the EU policies of social cohesion which seeks to provide access to decent and sanitary housing for all does depend on a minimum legal protection of the citizen from arbitrary eviction by the provision of explicit (if bounded) legal rights to security of tenure.

Market operations often prevent access for vulnerable groups to adequate and affordable housing. Economic restructuring impacts on the labour market exclusion of particular disadvantaged groups. This exclusion is compounded by housing market constraints that limit the amount and cost of housing in regionally and locally determined housing markets. Chapter Three examines the way in which the housing market operates in a changing European economy and evaluates its limitations in providing access to housing for vulnerable groups.

Access to housing requires a supply of housing sufficient to meet the needs of all households – or at least that there is a reasonable balance between supply and demand and no long-term shortages. Changes in the governance of housing and the organisational structures related to housing provision and management may therefore affect access to housing generally and for vulnerable groups in particular. The changing role of the state has had a major impact on the role of key housing providers (local authorities, housing associations) and the relationship between agencies (regulatory framework, nomination agreements). Three aspects of the policies and practices of government and housing institutions (at local, regional and national levels) may deny the ability of low-income groups to gain access to housing: first, the impact of subsidy and social protection systems and housing allowances on affordable housing costs for low-income groups; second, the effect of national policies on particular groups (for example, the young, single people); third, the need to develop integrated policies and procedures to meet the multi-dimensional needs of vulnerable groups in the housing market. These issues form the basis for discussion in Chapter Four.

The aim to provide access to housing for all citizens is an important principle in the context of the recent reforms that have been occurring in European systems of social welfare and health. The objective is complementary to policies which have led to the closure of large-scale long-stay institutions and the shift to the delivery of care services within the community. In this context access to housing for all implies that adequate and affordable support will be available to enable people with support needs to sustain a tenancy and to live independently in the community. Although these topics are the subject of detailed discussion elsewhere (Edgar et al, 2000), some of the key policy issues in relation to access to housing for vulnerable groups are also reflected upon in Chapter Four.

While Chapters Three and Four consider two of the three interrelated and overlapping pathways into housing – the market and redistribution through the state (such as subsidised social housing) – the importance of social networks and reciprocal relationships within the sphere of civil society form the subject matter of Chapter Five. Here also some consideration is given to the 'agency' of vulnerable people themselves, to the manner in which they are forced to rely on their own resources and capabilities.

Innovative approaches to open access to housing for particular vulnerable groups and policies and programmes to tackle housing exclusion are examined in Chapter Six. These issues also require consideration of partnership and inter-agency working. This is occurring, albeit often in an ad hoc and piecemeal fashion, in relation to housing provision, programmes for the homeless, inter-sectoral projects or to programmes of social inclusion. This examination is framed within the common objectives of the European strategy to fight poverty and social exclusion and draws examples from all the member states. A second aspect of the approach to opening access to housing for vulnerable groups includes evaluation of approaches designed to enable the participation of excluded people in the development and implementation of actions to help them. This involves traditional structures of housing advice, ethnic minority housing associations, self-help structures as well as more innovative approaches. In relation to the latter, limited available evidence means that its elucidation must await further, more focussed research.

Notes

[1] These figures are of course approximations. They are the products of the amalgamation of figures derived from the individual member states of the EU. These national figures are themselves best estimates, the result sometimes of extrapolations from often small sample surveys. The aggregate figures also disguise national differences in the definition of homelessness and housing vulnerability.

[2] The information on homelessness contained in the NAPs/incl is generally poor. Whenever indicators are available they tend to reflect administrative concerns and outputs (people dealt with by homelessness services) instead of focusing on outcomes.

[3] The issue of immigration and homelessness will be the subject of a forthcoming publication. While the issue of access to housing is clearly central to the integration of immigrants and should be part of admission procedures in all European countries, the analysis of housing vulnerable groups in this book, while intermittently touching on the topic, does not explicitly include immigrants.

[4] A previous FEANTSA publication (Avramov, 1995) focused on the issues relating to security of tenure. The research tended to concentrate on the financial and, especially, legal and juridical aspects of insecurity of tenure. Models of good practice were mainly considered in relation to the prevention of eviction.

TWO

The right to housing and access to housing in the European Union

Introduction: the right to housing

In philosophical literature, rights are commonly discussed in terms of abstract categories such as freedom, security and dignity. These, it is claimed, are universal and inalienable rights, attributable to all as a consequence of being human[1]. These are the rights enshrined and elaborated in the 30 articles of the 1948 Universal Declaration of Human Rights[2]. Considered alongside these universal rights, the right to housing can be regarded as a 'secondary' right, part of what Amartya Sen (1992, 1999)[3] calls a 'capability set' (along with adequate nourishment, proper clothing, minimal education, and so on) that every individual requires to permit attainment of these universal rights and thus the development of capacities as a species being; that is, as a dignified and free human being who "shapes his or her own life in cooperation and reciprocity with others" (Nussbaum, 2000, p 72).

Jeremy Waldron (1993) develops these themes in an examination of the links between homelessness and freedom. His basic argument is that humans, as embodied entities, need a private and secure location in which to carry out necessary and quotidian functions such as sleeping, washing, reproducing, socialising and so forth. In modern western (European) society such a location is typically secured by a 'right to housing'. Homeless people, by definition, are unable to access adequate housing of their own and societal property rules forbid access (without permission) to the private property (houses) of others. Homeless people are thereby 'denied' a safe and secure location for human functioning. The alternative location for homeless people, for human functioning, is public space. However, access to public space has been progressively restricted as a consequence of its increasing 'militarisation' (Davis, 1992): the social control of public space excludes certain functions, especially those of a personal and private nature, as well as socially undesirable people such as the homeless. Homelessness, in Waldron's argument, is not just a denial of a right to housing. Rather, it is a denial of the basic human right to a location, of access to 'somewhere' for basic human functioning and thereby a denial of freedom (opportunity and autonomy of action), of security (individual welfare and safety) and of dignity (respect)[4].

Homelessness breaks the links with 'normal' society, introducing a degree of social isolation and social disqualification, inhibiting access to a range of rights available, as a matter of course, to others in society. As a recent UN-Habitat document observed:

> Homelessness is not only the most severe violation of housing rights, it also reflects a status where all aspects of universally accepted human rights are open to abuse, violation and [non] fulfilment. Whichever definition of homelessness is used, persons suffering from this status are, to a large extent, excluded from opportunities enjoyed by most other members of society. (UNCHS, 2001, p 7)

However, capabilities, such as the access to housing, are not just instrumental in the pursuit of other objectives, they have value in themselves, in "making the life that includes them fully human" (Nussbaum, 2000, p 74). Similarly, Somerville and Chan (2002) point out that, through access to adequate and appropriate housing, an individual attains both self-esteem and societal respect. Homelessness, and the institutionalised, often disrespectful, treatment of those at risk of homelessness, strips away an individual's dignity, thereby effectively reducing his or her functioning capacity as a human being. For homeless people, the condition of homelessness also has real material consequences in bringing tangible hardships and in threatening "epidemiological security" (O'Flaherty, 1996, p 27) by increasing vulnerability to disease and ill health and the risk of premature death.

Progressing the concept of rights beyond the rhetorical requires recognition of the notion that rights imply a social relationship, a contract between individuals and society (a social group), in effect the acceptance of certain societal obligations with regard to ensuring that individual rights are valued and protected. The protection of the right of an individual to housing is the kind of right that entails not just the absence of certain actions, or constraints on certain activities on the part of other members of society (though these might be required). Rather, it necessarily involves active intervention – the establishment of "a positive infrastructure" (Somerville and Chan, 2001, p 5), and "institutional structures" (O'Neill, 1996, quoted in King, 2001, p 5). In a similar vein, Nussbaum argues that the articulation of capabilities – such as the right to housing – provides the underpinnings of basic political principles that can be embodied in constitutional guarantees. Furthermore, she argues that the structure of social and political institutions should be shaped with a view to promoting threshold levels of human capabilities. Below a certain level – a threshold – of capability, a person, in any given society, may not be able to "live in a truly human way" (Nussbaum, 2000, p 74)

The right to housing – the international context

> Everyone has the right to a standard of living adequate for the health and wellbeing of himself and his family, including food, clothing, housing and medical care and necessary social services.... (Universal Declaration of Human Rights, 1948, Article 25)

The right to housing is enshrined in several international agreements, rather perfunctorily in the 1948 Human Rights Declaration and more substantially in the agreement of the Second UN Conference on Human Settlements (Habitat II) held in Istanbul in 1996[5]. At the international level perhaps the most significant articulation of the right to housing is found in Article 11(1) of the 1976 International Covenant on Economic, Social and Cultural Rights (ICESCR), a covenant now endorsed by 140 countries. Here the right to housing is included as part of the larger right to an adequate standard of living. Under international human rights law, however, the right to adequate housing is understood to be an independent, freestanding right. This point was clarified in December 1991 when the UN Committee on Economic, Social and Cultural Rights adopted General Comment no 4 on the Right to Adequate Housing by a unanimous vote. This comment provides an authoritative interpretation of what housing rights actually mean in legal terms under international law. It provides a benchmark against which the situation in any one country can be compared, allowing a judgement to be made as to whether a country's government is acting in full compliance with the rights and obligations arising from the 1976 Covenant[6].

The international forum whose proceedings and activities have the most detailed consideration of housing issues is undoubtedly the UN Centre on Human Settlement (Habitat). The key issue of the 1996 Habitat meeting at Istanbul, for example, was the right to adequate housing. Thirty-three of the 241 paragraphs of the Istanbul Agreement and Habitat Agenda refer to housing and/or human rights. Paragraph 61 of the agenda identifies the actions and commitments of governments and other agencies needed to "promote, protect and ensure the full and progressive realisation of the right to adequate housing" (UNCHS, 1996, para 61). The June 2001 meeting of Habitat (sometimes known as Istanbul +5) reaffirmed the commitments of the Istanbul meeting and established the UN Human Settlement Programme (UN-Habitat). This programme, which draws on cooperation with the Office of the High Commissioner for Human Rights, is designed explicitly to promote housing rights through awareness campaigns, to develop benchmarks and monitoring systems, and to initiate projects.

While the concept of the 'right to housing' is now widely recognised, few governments have taken the required steps to ensure that all residents of their countries enjoy that right. As the position paper on housing rights of Habitat 2001 suggests, the norms and principles "contained in international instruments have not been sufficiently reflected in national legislative and institutional frameworks" (UNCHS, 2001, p 4). Even though the right to adequate housing figures more prominently in legislation in EU countries than elsewhere in the world, the EU and its constituent member states are no exception in this respect. This point was recognised recently by the EU working group implementing the Habitat Agenda:

> The right to adequate housing has advanced more slowly in practice than in law. (EU Working Group, 2000, p 26)

Indeed it is arguable that even in some of those countries where a right to housing has been established in the national constitution, the practice of that right is most limited (for example, Portugal, Belgium).

The European Union and the right to housing

While there is a plethora of resolutions, protocols, and instruments produced over the past five decades at the European level which deal explicitly or implicitly with the right to housing[7], the EU has no direct competence regarding issues of housing policy. Social issues, of which housing is a component part, are subject to the subsidiarity principle. All attempts to develop European-wide social policies have been frustrated by a combination of the legal limitations of EU competence enshrined in the founding Treaty of Rome (1957), and by the outright hostility of some member states. Each of these obstacles were clearly to be seen in a 1998 ruling of the European Court of Justice. Following an action initiated by the UK, the court confirmed that in the field of social policy only 'non-significant' actions – defined as those that do not interfere with policy arrangements of member states – can be legally executed by the EU.

Despite these restrictions, social and political issues, especially that of social cohesion, have increasingly been recognised since the early 1970s by the European Community (EC) as issues that cannot be ignored. Steadily, and with increasing frequency, social issues have been taken up in policy debates. This broadening of horizons is the result of two interrelated developments. First, an understanding and acceptance that economic decisions have negative, as well as positive, social and political consequences; that is, they impact unevenly across European regions and through European society. Second, the EC has expanded from a base in relatively homogeneously developed countries with continental welfare regimes, to embrace liberal, social democratic and most recently formative regimes of southern Europe. The EC is now characterised by an altogether greater diversity in which social and spatial, as well as economic, uneven development is clearly manifest. As the EC moves towards ever closer economic integration and contemplates further expansion into Eastern Europe, an explicit concern with social and political issues has become increasingly apparent. The emergence of the concepts of a 'social Europe' and 'European citizenship' is symptomatic (Leibfried and Pierson, 1994; Pinder, 1998).

An early indication of a growing involvement of the EC in social issues was the initiation in 1974-94 of the 'Poverty Programme', a series of three investigations into the relationship between economic cycles and variations in standards of living (Room, 1999). During the 1970s and 1980s the social concerns of the EC began to crystallise the concept of social exclusion and social cohesion. However, it was not until 1989 that the Council of Ministers passed a resolution dealing explicitly with social exclusion which lead, in 1990, to the establishment of the European Observatory on National Policies for Combating Social Exclusion. Concerns about social issues were also manifest in debates in the then DGV and DG XII[8] which led to the amendment of the objectives of the structural funds to include an explicit commitment to combat social exclusion and the incorporation of social exclusion research within the 4th framework.

In 1988 the Community Charter for Fundamental Social Rights of Workers was formulated in an explicit attempt to heighten awareness and to stimulate national action on poverty and exclusion. The charter included references to equal opportunities, sex discrimination and the rights of older people. In a diluted form this charter was incorporated as a protocol in the 1993 Maastricht Treaty. While this protocol fell short of the original intentions, its acceptance was indicative of a growing concern with poverty and social disadvantage on the part of most member states in the run up to monetary union.

In a separate but parallel and influential development, in 1994 the Council of Europe commissioned a substantial pan-European study of social exclusion among its 41 member countries, entitled *Human dignity and social exclusion* (Corden and Duffy, 1998; Room, 1999, pp 166-74). The Council of Europe, unrestrained by the economic orientation of the EC had already demonstrated an early concern with social issues. The Council's Social Charter of 1961, for example, spelt out a number of fundamental rights for workers and citizens of Europe, overtly referring the rights of the family, mothers and children to social, legal and economic protection. These concerns were reinforced and strengthened in a 1996 revision of the charter which came into force in July 1999. The revision introduced new clauses which included the right of protection against poverty and social exclusion, protection for the rights of women, children and the disabled and, in the first explicit recognition at the European level, the right to housing. Article 31 committed the signatories to the charter to promote access to housing of an adequate standard, to prevent and reduce homelessness with a view to its gradual elimination and to make the price of housing accessible to those without adequate resources (Council of Europe, 1996; FEANTSA, 1996)[9].

While the ability of the European Commission and European Parliament to effectively and directly intervene in housing issues has been constrained by their limited competence with regard to social policy formulation, Chapman and Murie (1996) have observed that housing has been drawn in on the back of concerns about social exclusion. In particular, it has indirectly benefited from the availability of structural funds for tackling urban regeneration, job training and work creation. They identify three ways in which the EU demonstrates responsibility for housing which fall short of formal policy intervention.

First, dialogue between member states has been sustained through the meetings of European housing ministers, which have taken place annually since 1989. These meetings – while ritualistically noting that housing policy is the exclusive responsibility of member states – allow for the exchange of experiences and the sharing of good practice. The Paris meeting in 2000 (the 12th in the series) debated the issue of 'public policies concerning access to housing' and the 13th gathering, held in Brussels and Charleroi in October 2001, considered the role of housing in reinforcing social cohesion. These meetings and other interactions have resulted in a series of reports by the European Commission on housing issues.

Second, Chapman and Murie (1996) argue that housing provision and management in Europe has been influenced by various pieces of legislation and regulatory guidelines relating to such issues as public procurement, health and safety, technical standards and consumer protection.

Third, they claim that housing policy has been influenced by the establishment of and the financial support (provided through DG Employment and Social Welfare – formerly DG V – for the most part) for a series of pan-European networks which focus on housing. These include CECODHAS (European Liaison Committee for Social Housing), OEIL (the European Organisation of Unions for Integration and Housing of Young Workers), FEANTSA (European Federation of National Organisations working with the Homeless) and EUROPIL (the European Federation for Social Assistance and Integration through Housing). The primary role of these organisations is as providers of information, but they also perform an important function in lobbying the European Commission and Parliament on housing and related issues (see also, Kleinman, 1996; Avramov, 1995, pp 153-9).

More recent activities indicate a continuing and indeed growing concern with social issues (including housing) on behalf of the EU. The social clauses of the 1999 Treaty of Amsterdam, albeit a disappointment in their restrictiveness, were a concrete demonstration by member states of both a recognition of and an increasing willingness to address the tension between economic goals and social outcomes. The Lisbon Summit in March 2000 outlined a strategy for the eradication of social exclusion. This was followed by the Nice Summit in December of the same year which proposed and approved the EU Charter on Fundamental Rights and initiated the programme of National Action Plans to fight poverty and social exclusion (NAPs/incl). While the charter brings together for the first time in an EU document civil, political, social and economic rights, it excludes any explicit reference to a right to housing. The agreed common objectives of the NAPs/incl, however, do include a commitment to promote 'access for all to decent and sanitary housing' and to the prevention of the risks of exclusion which includes homelessness. While such developments are to be welcomed, it is appropriate to note the linguistic slippage from the bold and unconstrained concept of a right to adequate housing to the more limited and restricted concept of a right *of access* to adequate housing. The terminology shift reduces the level of commitment from provision to opportunity.

The right to housing – the national context

> Since the mid-1980s, the homeless have assumed a highly visible presence in
> the public areas of EU cities. The problem is not a new one, but has taken on
> a new dimension, especially because extreme forms of poverty are unanimously
> judged to be unacceptable in a society of plenty. The position and living
> conditions of homeless people are everywhere viewed as an affront to human
> rights. (Committee of the Regions, 1999, p 4)

All EU member states have signed up to the 1948 Universal Declaration of
Human Rights and have ratified the 1976 International Covenant on Economic,
Social and Cultural Rights. This suggests that, formally at least, they recognise
the right to adequate accommodation as a fundamental human right, as an
essential element in ensuring respect for human dignity. Yet, as Avramov (1995,
p 158) indicates, throughout the EU, there is a "lack of explicit recognition of
the right to housing as an individual entitlement". It is certainly the case that
the manner in which the concept of housing rights have been incorporated in
national political systems and legislation varies substantially from country to
country and is hedged around with considerable ambiguity. Belgium, Finland,
the Netherlands, Portugal, Spain and Sweden are the only countries where the
concept of housing rights has been incorporated in national constitutions.
This, of course, does not necessarily mean that it has the force of law. France
and Belgium have specific laws, *Loi Besson* and *Loi Onkelinx* respectively,
formulated, in part, round the concept of rights. In Austria, Germany, and
Luxembourg, however, housing rights are merely referenced in various strands
of national legislation. The UK and Ireland do not explicitly acknowledge the
right to housing, but both have housing legislation which focuses specifically
on the problems of homelessness. In the UK, local authorities are required by
law to provide shelter for certain priority categories of people, while in Ireland
they are responsible for simply monitoring levels of homelessness and drawing
up housing priorities. Italy's 1978 decentralisation law devolves housing
responsibilities to regional authorities, and Greece's 1951 housing code – while
not imposing a legal requirement – sets minimum standards of decent housing
and establishes financial mechanisms for helping homeless people (Harvey, 1993).
In Denmark it is argued that existing housing and social policies do such a
good job in catering for housing needs, that there is no need for legislation to
explicitly cover the right to housing (Tosics and Erdösi, 2002).

In a recent overview of housing in the EU, the Committee of the Regions,
noting the uneven commitment to housing rights among member states, argued
that housing "is the first factor enabling an individual to set out on a process of
social and vocational integration", and called upon European institutions "to
give further consideration to the principle of the right to adequate
accommodation" (Committee of the Regions, 1999, p 13). The appeal of a
rights approach, which conceives of housing as a central component of a
'capability set' essential for human dignity, is that it is indeed inclusive: regardless

of status or circumstances, a person's right to housing is established by the very fact of being human. While the sentiments of the housing ministers expressed at their recent (2001) meetings in Paris and Charleroi, and the acknowledged housing objectives of the NAPs/incl have gone some way to introduce the language of rights into the European debate, the likelihood of the adoption of a European housing rights agenda remains remote. However, following the Treaty of Amsterdam, the Nice Summit and the adoption of the 'soft' approach of the open method of policy coordination, subsidiarity is no longer viewed – if it ever was – as merely a division of jurisdictions. Under the rubric of subsidiarity the EC's task in social matters is seen as the deployment of "the most suitable array of resources to support and supplement the actions of individual member states ... [with a focus on] ... encouraging cooperation and social dialogue" (Mayes et al, 2001, p 69). In promoting the dissemination of good practice and benchmarking, the open method of policy coordination will ensure that rights continue to provide a backdrop to policy considerations.

While European convergence on housing rights may be remote, for more pragmatic reasons, housing issues are, in Kleinman's (2002) view, the area of social concern most likely to experience a degree of increased European interest in the immediate future. First, he argues, there is now a network of vocal and effective interest groups and institutions associated with housing at the European level (FEANTSA, CECODHAS, among others) that will continue to press for a role in the EU. Second, housing lies at the intersection of economic and social policy. Housing was only ever partially decommodified. The private market (owner occupation together with private renting) – even during those decades when social housing provision was in its ascendancy – has always been a major provider of accommodation and, with the rapid (re)commodification of housing – the transfer of social housing to the private sector – now taking place in all European countries, its economic importance is set to increase. Housing, and particularly the private housing market, as a key component of all national economies (Ball, 2002; Glomm and John, 2001; *The Economist*, 2002), overlaps with economic interests of EU institutions, coming within the scope of their competence in areas such as economic and monetary policies, competition policy and promotion of the single market. As Kleinman (2002, p 350) points out, European institutions are directly involved in housing through a concern with a number of issues, particularly: the regulation of mortgages; levels of spending on housing by both governments and households; the way housing finance affects public sector expenditure; and competition in the construction industry. EU institutions are also drawn into housing as a consequence of broader considerations linked with the recently emerged discourse on social exclusion; a socially cohesive Europe is seen as an essential ingredient for an economically competitive Europe (Room, 1995; Edgar et al, 2000, pp 13-31). It is no coincidence that the Lisbon and Nice summits of 2000, which proclaimed the objective of making Europe a globally competitive, knowledge-based economy, were also deeply concerned with issues of social exclusion, especially as it relates to employment and housing. An aspect of the open method of policy coordination is the encouragement of 'activation', which tries to create more immediate links between welfare and work:

> Social policy is seen as a potentially productive factor that may help to stimulate growth and employment. Growth and employment on the other hand are often seen as serving social policy purposes in that both facilitate the inclusion of marginalised people in the labour market. (Begg et al, 2001, p 6)

Precisely because housing bridges the divide between social policy and economic policy, the potential for EU level development is greater than for many other areas of social policy.

Vulnerability and access to housing in the European Union

The ability of Europeans to exercise a right of access to adequate and secure housing is contingent upon inclusion in the economic, social, and political structures of individual nations and of European society. Housing vulnerability is constituted by exclusion or threat of exclusion from these structures. While the majority of European residents may be adequately housed, for significant numbers – estimates vary – access to adequate housing is an issue of daily and intense personal concern. For these individuals and households, their condition of housing vulnerability and exclusion is delimited and distinguished by one or more circumstances:

- the occupation of poor accommodation lacking structural integrity or basic amenities;
- the absence of security of tenure and threat of eviction or harassment;
- temporary residence in emergency or short-term accommodation;
- homelessness.

For these individuals and households, the agencies and institutions of housing provision (principally the private market and the state) have proved incapable of ensuring access to adequate housing. The vulnerable are those individuals and groups who find themselves in the interstices between the operational frameworks of these agencies. Housing vulnerability is, in its broadest sense, the condition of those who are unable to gain access to adequate housing through conventional and established 'channels of acquirement' (Sen, 1999; Waldron, 2000).

Some individuals and groups are more susceptible to housing vulnerability than others, due to socially attributed and inherited characteristics (race, disability, gender, sexual orientation, and so on) or life course events (unemployment, family break up, domestic violence, onset of major illness or infirmity). This situation reflects enduring deficiencies in the social fabric and structures of society. However, the precise characteristics of those who comprise the vulnerable at particular times and places are not predetermined. Housing vulnerability has a shifting constituency, reflecting the direct and indirect impact of changing economic circumstances, social trends and political climates, as well as the changing roles and responsibilities of the main agents and institutions of housing provision.

In recent decades, changing economic, social and political formations have not only aggravated housing vulnerability among traditionally vulnerable individuals, they have also created new vulnerabilities. For example, economic change associated with deindustrialisation and the creation of a flexible labour force has produced unemployment and housing vulnerability among those who previously enjoyed security of employment. Social and demographic changes linked with, among other developments, the demise of the male breadwinner household have exposed some women to the vagaries of the labour market constraining their ability to form and sustain independent households. Additionally, changing political circumstances have diluted the postwar consensus on the role of welfare, leading to new categories of housing vulnerability among groups as diverse as young people and asylum seekers, while the rise of a new political right (such as List Pim Fortuyn in the Netherlands, Le Pen in France, the BNP in Britain, anti-immigrant groups in Belgium, and Haider in Austria) threatens the already tenuous rights of some immigrant, ethnic and religious minorities.

The shifting constituency of housing vulnerability reflects also the transformations wrought by these same changed economic, social and political conditions on the responsibilities and functions of the main agencies and institutions of housing provision – the state and the private market.

Institutional provision and access to housing

All EU member states have relatively sophisticated private housing markets which respond with varying degrees of efficiency to housing demands. In each country this market is paralleled by highly variable and often complex mixes of housing and social welfare policies providing combinations of 'bricks and mortar' subsidies and individual and household allowances which attempt to compensate, at least in part, for the deficiencies of the market. Yet, as the persistence of homelessness and the large numbers of inadequately housed people in all EU countries testify, the gap between what this mix of market and welfare promises, and what it actually delivers, is palpable.

The 'channels of acquirement' (Sen, 1999) through which people access housing in Europe are defective: they fail to ensure the access of all to adequate housing; they fall well short of ensuring the levels of human dignity embodied in the concept of 'right to housing', and they are defective when judged by the standards of social justice encapsulated in the concept of social inclusion. Homelessness and inadequate housing represent some of the most visible and extreme manifestations of exclusion, in that they are symptomatic not just of the absence of shelter, but are also indicative of a combination of social dislocation and marginalisation. As Somerville has observed, echoing some of the insights of Jeremy Waldron's analysis:

> ... social exclusion through housing happens if the effect of the housing processes is to deny certain social groups control over their daily lives or impair enjoyment of wider citizenship rights. (Somerville, 1998, p 772)

The already flawed ability of the blending of market and state to ensure access to adequate housing for all of Europe's population has been further tested in recent years. Since the mid-1970s, the welfare state, which underpins the provision of social housing, has been subject to a series of external and internal pressure which have brought about major changes and may even threaten its future survival. Globalisation and the apparent inexorable demand for economic competitiveness, technological change, restructured labour markets, plus demographic and social changes and shifts in political ideology have all called into question the traditional forms of the delivery of welfare. These transformative societal changes have damaged, to a greater or lesser degree, the ability of the welfare states of all EU countries to adequately service traditional target populations and have presented these welfare structures with new demands unforeseen when they first emerged after the Second World War. Postwar welfare states were formed in a period of traditional families (male breadwinner: women carers at home), low unemployment and lower life expectancy. Such welfare systems were unprepared for burgeoning demands from traditional target groups and were not designed for, and have been found wanting in coping with, or adapting to, the new demands thrown up by economic and social change. The structural and organisational inadequacies of welfare states – which includes their ability to provide access to adequate housing – have been exacerbated by a crisis of public funding that casts doubt on the continuing capacity and, perhaps, willingness of governments to deliver quality welfare provision.

The changing role of the state is sometimes encapsulated in the term 'hollowing out' (Jessop, 1994). This involves the divesting of state responsibilities 'upwards' to supra-national organisations such as the EU, the 'downward' transfer of responsibilities to local government and quasi-state organisation, and the dispersion 'outwards' to NGOs and the voluntary sector, as well as to private, for-profit enterprises. The scale of this hollowing out process varies from country to country and is not, necessarily, linearly cumulative in that the state sometimes claims back powers and responsibilities (Rhodes, 1994). Further, the significance of the hollowing out process is disputed – does it, as some claim, lead to the establishment of a 'shadow state' (Wolch, 1989) whereby, through monitoring and regulation and indeed funding, the state effectively retains control over the intent and direction of these alternative agencies? Or does it represent something altogether more fundamental, the surrender of state power and control, allowing other ideologies, whether of the laissez-faire market or those of civil society, free reign (Bryson et al, 2002)? Both tendencies can be identified across EU member states and indeed in regional variations within individual countries.

The retrenchment of the welfare state in EU member states over the course of the last few decades provides a trenchant manifestation of the hollowing out process as it relates to social policy. Though uneven in its impact, all European societies, under the umbrella of a neoliberal political ethos, have experienced the sloughing-off of once well defined state responsibilities to the private sector and to the voluntary sector; to the market and to civil society. Hollowing out has set in train a reversal of those processes of 'decommodification' and 'defamilialisation' which Esping-Andersen (1990, 1999) and others (such as Sainsbury, 1996) used in their fashioning of welfare regime typologies. In relation to housing policy, the retrenchment of the welfare state is apparent in two tendencies. First, in the curtailment of 'bricks and mortar' subsidies to non-state providers of subsidised housing and the curbing of expenditure on benefit payments to vulnerable households. Second, retrenchment has been apparent in the withdrawal of the state from the direct provision of social housing. The overall impact has been, on the one hand, to boost market involvement in providing access to housing and, on the other, to encourage the resurgence of not-for-profit organisations in the form of quasi-state or charitable or voluntary housing agencies (see Chapter Four of this volume).

The increasing role of the market is justified on the grounds that rising incomes for some sections of the population renders the need for social housing less essential and that peoples' apparently increasing preference for home ownership is best served by the private market. Further, it is argued that savings made on housing expenditure by shifting housing provision to the private sector release state finances to invest in other aspects of welfare such as pensions, health and education. While the housing needs of those households with secure and stable incomes can perhaps be catered for by the private market, those of households on low or no incomes are clearly not. As O'Flaherty (1996) demonstrates, in a somewhat quirky if neglected study of homelessness in the US, commodification exacerbates housing vulnerability for significant sectors of the population. O'Flaherty's analysis shows how, even in conditions of national economic growth and prosperity, the market fails to generate conditions which lead to a decrease in housing vulnerability. In such conditions, the demand from increasingly affluent households applies a downward pressure on available housing, drawing into the formal market housing previously considered marginal. As marginal, previously low cost housing becomes desirable, rents and prices move up and poorer households are deprived of the opportunities for cheap, affordable accommodation. Faced with decisions on how to spend scarce disposable income, low-income households, in such circumstances, opt to forego housing. Poverty and homelessness, O'Flaherty argues, are relatively unaffected by the movement of markets. The poorest segments of society remain vulnerable to homelessness in conditions of boom as in conditions of stagnation and recession[10]. The commodification of housing can also exacerbate housing vulnerability in other ways. In conditions of housing market inflation many middle income households are priced out of the market and mortgage defaulting and repossession increases, while housing market deflation leads to problems of negative equity (see Chapter Three of this volume).

The flip side of commodification is a decreasing – or stagnant at best – role for the state in promoting and providing affordable social housing. Again the process, while not uniform, is apparent to a greater or lesser extent in all EU countries. For example, state withdrawal from direct social housing provision is evident in the limited amounts of further investment in existing stock and in the virtual cessation of investment in new stock[11]. It is also apparent in the disposal of stock by municipalities and local authorities through privatisation (such as the right to buy in the UK) and transfer to not-for-profit housing companies and associations (as occurs in Sweden). The result has been the residualisation of remaining municipal and council properties (disproportionately in the worst condition and the least preferred), and the ghettoisation of residents and the stigmatisation of neighbourhoods (see Chapter Three of this volume). Municipal and council housing is increasingly seen as welfare housing, residual housing for those who are unable to access housing elsewhere; it is what Taylor (1979) described as 'difficult to let and difficult to get out of' – it is housing of the last resort. Housing vulnerability is exacerbated by this process in that residents in residualised municipal social housing are often trapped and unable to access better quality housing, while the access options for other low income households and homeless households are curtailed as a consequence of diminished supply.

Civil society and access to housing

Paralleling the withdrawal of the state from direct involvement, there has been a fragmentation of social housing provision in the form of a resurgence in civil society agencies as alternative suppliers. For example, in Britain, housing companies and housing associations are now the main – and in some regions the only – providers of new social housing, as they have long been in some countries in mainland Europe[12]. The functions and roles of these not-for-profit organisations are complex. Some are so dependent on state funding that they operate as quasi-state organisations performing a state directed role at arms length, their actions called to account through regulation and periodic monitoring, effectively contributing to what some have identified as a 'shadow state' (Wolch, 1990; Warrington, 1995). Other, mostly charitable, providers, such as religious and confessional associations in Mediterranean countries, though not free of regulation, operate much more independently, determining their own goals and objectives and sometimes providing innovative services (see Edgar et al, 1999). In that all these agencies explicitly target households in need, access to housing for vulnerable groups is, arguably, enhanced by this proliferation of providers. However, as state funding for the quasi-state and other organisations is squeezed under the imperatives of retrenchment, so the ability of these organisations to provide access is curtailed. In pursuing the goal of providing access to adequate housing for vulnerable groups, such organisations increasingly find themselves caught between the demands of financial viability and the threat of insolvency (see Chapter Four of this volume). While the charitable and independent sector pursues admirable objectives, especially with regard to specific targets (for example, almshouses in Britain catering for older people; see Bryson et al, 2002) its impact, while not trivial, in enhancing access for vulnerable groups is restricted by its overall size.

The exclusivity of the market, together with the contraction and fragmentation of social housing operating under increasing financial stringency, has forced many among those experiencing housing vulnerability to fall back on informal channels of access. In a reversal of the defamilialisation process, whereby the welfare state took on the caring role traditionally performed in the extended and nuclear families, the 'survival strategies' of those experiencing housing vulnerability display some of the best aspects of reciprocity, with family and friends providing temporary and emergency accommodation (albeit frequently in already overcrowded and inadequate housing). However, informal solutions to the problems of housing vulnerability also have their dark side involving dependence on the exploitative provision of overpriced, insecure and illegal accommodation in slums and shanty towns (see Chapter Five of this volume).

The existence of these exploitative situations is the most dramatic representation of deep-seated housing vulnerability in the EU and demonstrates clearly the bankruptcy of the housing rights debate currently being conducted at EU level. It also, however, offers that debate its major challenge – the challenge to translate the debate into policy and to operationalise the concept of the right to housing by providing adequate housing for all on the grounds of social justice and equity as well as social cohesion. Yet, in that housing vulnerability is not a new phenomenon, reliance of the vulnerable on top-down solutions to the problem of access to adequate housing would be misplaced. The vulnerable themselves require empowerment – not in the 'weak' sense of training and integration, but in the 'strong', more powerful sense of organisation for campaigning and lobbying. The history of social movements suggests that only when bottom-up pressures are sufficiently applied, will top-down talk of rights be translated into effective action.

Conclusion

In an evaluation of the extent of change in the welfare state brought about by late 20th century economic, social and political transformations, Taylor-Gooby (2000, p 187) concludes that, "the impact has varied across countries and from one welfare regime to another" and that there is little evidence to suggest that "distinctive [welfare] regimes have shown any tendency to converge". Rather, he argues, they have "displayed considerable resilience under the impact of current pressures". Nordic countries, long associated with a social democratic, universalistic welfare regime, seem to be handling things best – a judgement reinforced by the analysis of Goodin et al (1999). However, Taylor-Gooby goes on to suggest that while "the welfare state has so far been relatively undamaged [it now faces] a more severe challenge than at any time in its 50-year history" (pp x-1) and that "there are strong indications that the path is now open to more radical reform" (p 187).

Taylor-Gooby's rather conservative conclusions with regard to the extent of change so far, emerge from an analysis focused on such traditional welfare issues as pensions, social spending, tax systems, labour market participation, and healthcare. Taylor-Gooby takes no account of housing. In that social housing has probably undergone more fundamental change than other sectors of welfare provision, it may be that housing can be seen as presenting these other sectors of welfare with an 'image of their own futures'.

The following chapters chart the impact of welfare state retrenchment on housing access for vulnerable groups in European society. With the withdrawal of the state, housing provision in Europe is increasingly determined on the basis of market principles. The adverse consequences for vulnerable groups who, for example, for want of the ability to pay are unable to access the market, is demonstrable in the persistent high levels homelessness in all EU countries. As a corollary to this shifting of the balance between the roles of the state and the market, a process of *re-familiarisation* can be identified: a revival in the role of civil society in providing informal, and sometimes illegal, alternative shelter for those who slip through the increasingly coarse-grained net of the state/ market nexus. In the final chapter of this volume we return explicitly to the issue of 'right to housing' to elaborate some aspects of what Ingrid Sahlin (2001) has referred to as a 'rights approach' to housing provision.

Notes

[1] Donnelly (1993) provides an overview. Depicted in these general terms, such rights remain rather formless and are clearly amenable to different social interpretations. There is an historic and ongoing debate on the concept of rights in the philosophical literature which overlaps with an equally prolific social and political literature debating issues of responsibility and obligation. See for example Rawls (1971); Dworkin (1977); MacIntyre (1985); Warnock (1992); Jordan (1996).

[2] Everyone, it declared, regardless of race, creed, gender or nationality, has: the right to equality of treatment; liberty and security of person; the right to nationality; privacy; freedom of movement; to work; the right of free expression; the right to an adequate standard of living; and participation in political and cultural life. These rights are still debated, contested and challenged (see the recent challenge mounted by Libya, in Mazower, 2002).

[3] See also Nussbaum (2000, especially pp 78-79) for a more exigent approach to the concept of capabilities. Nussbaum also draws a parallel between her work and that of

Sen's and with the 'primary goods' approach that Rawls (1971) proposed in the elaboration of his 'theory of justice'.

[4] The 'space entitlements' perspective, adopted by the UNCHS (1996), implicitly at least, reflects on some of the same concerns as those identified by Waldron (1993).

[5] The right to adequate housing is enshrined in many international documents. See CHORE (2000) for a comprehensive list.

[6] Adequate housing is defined in the covenant as housing which is characterised by accessibility; security of tenure; availability of services; affordability; habitability; appropriate and secure location; and cultural adequacy (CHORE, 2000).

[7] Regional Instruments include:

- European Convention on Human Rights and Fundamental Freedoms – ECHR (1950), Article 8(1); Protocol no 1 and no 4 to ECHR;
- European Social Charter (1961), Articles 16, 19 and 31;
- European Convention on the Legal Status of Migrant Workers (1977), Article 13;
- Community Charter of Fundamental Social Rights (1989), Article 29;
- European Parliament Resolution on Shelter for Homeless in the European Community (1987), Paragraphs 4-8;
- Final Act of Helsinki (1975) CSCE;
- The Vienna concluding Document (1989), Principle 14;
- Document of the Copenhagen Meeting of the Conference on Human Dimension of the CSCE (1990), Article 23;
- Revised European Social Charter (1961) of the Council of Europe (1996);
- Nice Summit of Heads of State – European Council approved a Charter of Fundamental Human Rights for the EU;
- National Action Plans to fight poverty and Social exclusion – adopted at the Lisbon Summit March 2000. Access for all to decent sanitary housing as well as basic services having regard to local circumstances (electricity, water, heating, and so on).

[8] The remit of DG V was employment, industrial relations and social affairs and it was responsible for the anti-poverty programmes; DG XII's remit was science, research and development.

[9] Only five of the 41 members of the Council of Europe have so far ratified this revised charter.

[10] O'Sullivan (2001) identifies similar tendencies in relation to recent trends in the Irish housing market.

[11] The recent investment in social housing in Denmark (Koch-Nielsen, 2001) and Ireland (O'Sullivan, 2001) are exceptional. And of course some countries such as Belgium have historically had little social housing to speak of (De Decker, 2001).

[12] In terms of stock size, local authorities in Britain remain, for the present, the largest social housing landlords.

THREE

Commodification and access to housing

The market within the housing market

In this chapter we use 'housing market' to refer to the private housing market which operates according to the principles of supply and demand, and includes privately rented and owner-occupied housing. We examine the way this market works in the wider and changing context of the European economy and evaluate its limitations in providing access to housing for vulnerable groups. We argue that in European society, access to housing through the marketplace can be seen as one of three interrelated and overlapping pathways into housing. The other two pathways[1] – redistribution through the state (for example, subsidised public housing) and reciprocal exchange (such as free lodging with relatives in exchange for other services) – are the subject matter of Chapters Four and Five of this volume.

Understanding the commodification of housing

The complex process of the commodification of housing refers to the increasing dominance of the market in the distribution of housing. This process is apparent, albeit unevenly, in all EU countries and reflects the withdrawal of the state from direct provision of housing. In this chapter we examine several facets of this process. First, we focus on two strongly interrelated processes that have a clear but indirect impact on the access to housing. These are, namely, the restructuring of the labour market and the concomitant socio-spatial logic of the new economic cycle of growth. Next we examine the emergence of new regional housing markets and the ways in which existing markets have been altered. This is followed by an examination of the widespread incentives for home ownership and the commodification of social housing which have emerged in nearly all European countries. Finally, we consider the ongoing deregulation and bifurcation of the private housing market. This chapter focuses on the ways in which these five trends contribute to the (re)production of a large number of inadequate and substandard dwellings which are occupied by the lowest income groups.

Restructured labour markets and the new logic of spatial organisation

An individual's access to housing through market exchange is dependent on the purchasing power of his or her household. This implies that the acquisition of decent housing is dependent on the ability to valorise productive capacity in the marketplace. An interpretation of the workings of the housing market cannot be understood without considering (from the household's point of view) the labour market and the structural interactions between the labour and the housing market. In capitalist societies, the labour market is not just a passive source of income maintenance, it is also important as a structural means of integration into society (Duffy, 1999).

The so-called post-Fordist labour market, which emerged in Europe during the last quarter of the 20th century, is characterised by four important structural changes, which are mutually linked: globalisation, flexibility, informality and polarisation. We shall discuss each of these trends briefly with a particular emphasis on the consequences for access to the housing market and the social production of homelessness.

The current process of globalisation of capitalist societies is not limited to the profit-led scaling up of enterprises, which seeks out cheap labour and other means of production across the world. Globalisation also includes the wide-ranging migration of people from the global periphery to the western core. The fact that most European states try to manage these migration flows by the inappropriate use of asylum procedures (Meert et al, 2002a) shows the clumsiness of most countries in dealing with the social and economic problems faced by these vulnerable groups in acquiring, inter alia, access to decent housing.

Closely linked to the ongoing process of globalisation, the post-Fordist organisation of the labour market entails a new cycle of growth within the capitalist economy that is based on 'flexibility' in capital, in infrastructure and in employment. Data from France, for instance, show that the share of temporary jobs has increased from 3.3% in 1983 to 11% in 1994 (Betton, 2001, p 8). This contrasts with the former period of Fordism which relied on a full-time, stable (often male) workforce and mass production for mass consumption. The current impact of globalisation leads to a flexible organisation of almost the whole economy, in which the decrease of job security is compensated for in the case of highly-educated executives by very well paid jobs. However, this flexibility in the labour market can have tragic consequences for lower income groups. The combination of low education levels and job insecurity leads to increasing income insecurity. In many labour intensive sectors, current working conditions are reverting to the situation of the working class in the 19th century (Kesteloot, 2002). In those situations where laws and other regulations relating to the formal labour market prevent the unlimited exploitation of labour, employers look to two alternatives: low wage countries and the local informal labour market. Before considering the question of the local informal labour market in depth, it is important to stress that this flexibility in the labour market has far-reaching consequences for the housing market. On the one hand, the combination of the flexible deployment of people in the production process and the downward pressure on wages is leading to increased income insecurity and, consequently, problems in securing access to adequate housing especially for the weakest income groups. On the other hand, a flexible labour market involving a continuous switch of occupiers in the housing market creates problems for landlords who prefer stable households that pay rent regularly with a minimum of administrative costs. In the case of substandard and inadequate housing requiring extensive refurbishment, the dumping of these dwellings on the informal housing market, where administrative and other legal obligations are ignored, is just one route by which landlords can deal with the inconveniences of frequently moving and marginalised employees.

These trends in the international labour market go hand in hand with the creation and development of an informal labour market. The current international migration trends, the increase of 'McJobs' and the need for flexibility, give rise to the creation of a local 'third world' economy in many European countries[2]. The need to slow down the rise in wages means that this process can be seen in the most labour intensive jobs and particularly when the production process does not allow some production to take place in low-income regions elsewhere in the world. This is particularly evident in the service sector, such as in cleaning and construction. Several European case-studies have shown that the informal organisation of the labour market is closely linked with the spatial organisation of the housing market (for example, see Body-Gendrot and Martiniello, 2000). This is apparent in the manner in which deprived neighbourhoods with low-income inhabitants are used as a large reservoir from which willing employees can be drawn. Such employees, it is assumed, will not make a fuss when wages are paid irregularly, or will do without pay during sickness or other enforced absences from work. It is also to be seen in the manner in which the housing market itself undergoes a process of informalisation, in order to provide shelter for low- and irregularly paid informal workers. For instance, Indian fruit pickers in strawberry regions of Belgium (De Decker and Meert, 2000a), or foreign immigrants working in the Andalusian Greenhouses in southern Spain, are housed in completely inadequate rented shacks (Cabrera, 2001). In Belgian cities such as Brussels, Antwerp and Ghent, there is evidence that, in the 1990s, households and individuals informally employed in construction and in the production of ready-to-wear clothing hired mattresses for monthly rents equivalent to €75-100 (Meert, 1998). Taking into account the European Federation of National Organisations working with the Homeless' (FEANTSA) broad definition of homelessness, it becomes clear that the interaction between the flexible labour market and the housing market, two basic pillars of society, produces particular forms of homelessness on a large scale.

Finally, as a result of the ongoing processes of globalisation, with its flexible, and sometimes informal, economy, western labour markets have developed a new hierarchical structure (Sassen, 1991). The robust Fordist labour market typified by a triangle with a wide base of blue-collar workers, a narrowing middle and a pointed top of high incomes, is disappearing fast. A new hourglass structure is emerging, characterised by a narrow middle caught between a wide base of so-called 'McJobs' and a wide top of high-salaried occupations. As a consequence of this new structure, upward social mobility for those at the bottom of the labour market is structurally impeded, hindering at the same time possibilities for access to the better segments of the housing market.

Gentrification and the reshaping of the urban landscape

The new modes of economic regulation associated with globalisation and post-Fordist capitalism have entailed major changes in the built environment of many European cities. This is especially so, but not only, in those which aspire to the status of world city – major interaction points in the global network of decision making and capital flows. Capitalism in the 21st century requires a new spatial organisation, a remaking of the urban landscape, with dramatic consequences for low-income residents (Harvey, 1989). There are two interrelated processes at work here. First, the reshaping of the commercial built environment of the central city; in other words, the construction of new hotels and other infrastructure to accommodate the 'flexible' executive, as he/she moves between world cities, and to attract 'footloose' international capital investment. The commercial regeneration of the urban environment has led to the large-scale exclusion of the weakest inhabitants in the urban housing market. It is in these central city areas that the majority of new international hotels, the new high-speed transport networks, the conference rooms and other post-Fordist artefacts are replacing the existing infrastructure of mixed-use neighbourhoods (including semi- and unskilled jobs as well as low-income housing). In this context, Pels' exhaustive reports on the housing market in the Grand Duchy of Luxembourg reveal the impact of such influences on its capital city. Here, even middle-class households are forced to leave the city because of rising prices and the ongoing transformation of dwellings into offices (Pels, 2001).

The second aspect of the emerging spatial structure of European cities, also leading to the exclusion of the weakest players in the housing market is linked to the selective building of dwellings for the highest income classes. The new flexible lifestyle, and related consumption patterns, of higher educated and well-paid senior executives and officials, goes hand in hand with a growing interest in centrally located urban neighbourhoods where they have easy access to transport systems, a variety of fine or exotic food, new cultural initiatives and other fashionable niches of the new economy. As a consequence, desirable central city locations, formerly occupied by deprived working class neighbourhoods, have attracted a lot of new interest. Typically through processes of speculation, these settings finally pass into the hands of private developers who construct new flats and dwellings, with the aim of maximising profits.

As a consequence of these gentrification processes, hundreds of thousands of cheap dwellings have disappeared in the EU during the last decade. In France it is estimated that, since the mid-1980s, only one in ten of the renovated low-budget dwellings of the private rental market were made accessible at a reasonable price after refurbishment, while each year about 100,000 cheap private dwellings disappeared from the market (Betton, 2001). In Austria, Schoibl (2001) reports that it is particularly the older housing units in the private housing market which have been targeted for refurbishment and redevelopment. Commercial estate agencies have bought up apartment houses in the central parts of cities and implemented so-called development programmes. Tenants in these old houses have been pushed out of their flats despite, in some instances, long-term tenancy agreements which, in principle, should make it illegal to remove them. Low-cost tenancies for low-income people have been replaced by high standard and expensive housing units (2001). In Denmark the effects of the national policy of urban renewal demonstrate clear, though delayed, gentrification effects, due in part to the eventual withdrawal of special housing benefits paid to some sitting tenants (Skifter Andersen, 2000; Nordgaard and Koch-Nielsen, 2001). In the initial phases, the state provided such benefits to sustain the social objectives of the urban renewal policy. However, after the abolishment of these specific interventions for employed people, 20% of the original residents were either expelled from their dwelling or chose to move because they found the dwelling too expensive (Skifter Andersen, 2000, p 130). Only pensioners and receivers of social benefits remained since they continued to receive housing benefit.

The impact of the new system of spatial organisation is not limited to the central city. Rather, it affects the entire city. Donzelot and Jaillet (1997) argue that European cities today are characterised by an increasing spatial segregation of the different classes. In contrast to the 19th century, when cities fulfilled the role of a forum where the working class and the bourgeois had to meet each other because of their interacting habitats, present-day post-Fordist cities are characterised as gated communities alongside large slum-like neighbourhoods which provides little opportunity of meeting or confrontation between the urban cohabitants. In other words, according to both Donzelot and Jaillet, we are witnessing at present the transition from 'dramaturgical' to 'topological' forms of urban organisation. While this general thesis has to be adjusted to take account of the specific and historically developed layouts of individual European cities, there is clear evidence throughout Europe of the increasing segregation and isolation of deprived urban neighbourhoods with inadequate and substandard housing. In Porto, for instance, social housing ghettos as well as the classical Portuguese slums in the metropolitan peripheries, built in inaccessible areas, are totally cut off from the rest of the city (Bruto da Costa and Baptista, 2001). However, this would seem to be an extreme case especially applicable to the southern European cities, in which the affluent households who need the city for work, leisure and shopping, have no direct contact with the poor who have been forced to live in the peripheral areas by prices. The situation is not so clear-cut in the case of Belgian cities, for example, (and also to some extent for British cities), where the affluent suburban households have to cross a poor inner-city belt around the city centre before they have access to work, leisure and shopping facilities (Kesteloot, 2002).

The question arises as to what extent, and how, this present-day segregated city is linked to the production and reproduction of inadequate and substandard housing. Musterd and Ostendorf's seminal collection of papers (1998) on urban segregation and the welfare state offers many arguments linking the segregation process with the emergence of large concentrations of inadequate and substandard housing areas in Europe's major cities. Murie (1998) has concluded, for instance, and mainly based on empirical work in Edinburgh, that increased spatial segregation goes hand in hand with a spatial concentration of poverty, exclusion from the labour market, housing tenure and a particular (imposed) residential location[3]. Therefore, high unemployment rates, low incomes and poor housing conditions coincide not only at the household level but also at the neighbourhood level. If we consider this observation along with the widespread and growing trend in home ownership as the pathway to improved housing, the prospects for these segregated and marginalised households, as well as the deprived neighbourhoods in which they concentrate, are not too good. Moreover, these neighbourhoods and their inhabitants are at the same time embedded in already existing and newly created regional patterns within national housing markets. Such regional housing markets are clearly related to the uneven and 'flexible' spread of new investments in the global economy, which in turn lead to the pressures on the real estate market we have been discussing and consequently to the related increase of high-standard housing areas for highly skilled executives. As it entails a regional diversity within a given national context of access to housing, this process of burgeoning new regional housing markets, the redrawing of existing ones and the consequences for the most marginalised households, merits our attention. This will form the next section, before we move on to consider in more detail the aspects of growing home ownership.

Access to housing and the growing dominance of the market

The housing landscape in any given country has an uneven morphology of rich and poor regions, areas of opportunity and areas of constraint. The regional housing markets that make up the national market are affected by macro-economic factors and national economic restructuring and, in turn, these influence regional competitiveness. They also emerge from regional and local differences in general welfare policy and housing policy. An understanding of access to housing must therefore reflect the positive and negative effects which regional housing markets can exert on housing choice. The effects of regional inequalities on housing opportunities for vulnerable households can persist in all economic circumstances, in areas of growth as well as in areas of decline, in highly urbanised economies as well as in more agrarian economies. This landscape of differential opportunity and access is a reflection not just of present day socio-economic and socio-political factors, but also of the historical pattern of housing provision. While this observation may be of more academic than policy interest, it does demonstrate the importance of time, and the lengthy timescales that may be needed, to reverse housing access problems. This view of housing access issues highlights the need to understand the impact at the local level that macro-economic factors, or nationally determined housing policies, can have on vulnerable households in different parts of the country. Comparative analysis at the local or neighbourhood level between countries is necessary if the impact of policy is to be understood.

Inequalities in regional housing markets can be the result of a range of factors related to housing and economics. A relative shortage of dwellings in regions of population growth will create access problems. Tenure structures, determined by historic building patterns and political factors, may be inappropriate to meet current patterns of demand. House prices relative to incomes may mean that housing subsidies, which are often determined centrally and applied in a regionally neutral manner, are ineffective in bringing housing costs within the means of lower income households in specific regions. Institutional structures distort the nature of housing provision. For example, the relative lack of social housing in rural areas may be a result of the absence of a housing association or municipal activity in those regions. Economic factors also influence the situation in that land prices and labour costs affect the relative costs of housing construction and can influence both housing demand, housing quality and housing tenure. The decisions and behaviours of tenants and prospective tenants can also distort the landscape of housing opportunity since individual migration decisions are influenced by economic, cultural and housing factors. These individual decisions in turn distort housing opportunities at the local level with, for example, migrants following previous migrants to the same destinations (Body-Gendrot and Martiniello, 2002). Equally, patterns of homelessness may be a reflection of the pattern of service provision for the homeless.

The impact of regional housing markets on the access to housing can be illustrated with several examples across the EU. They indicate that historical patterns as well as recently operating structures and trends are crucial to understand their existence and their impact on access to housing, especially for the weakest players in the private market. We shall discuss three examples.

Finland

Regional differences in the Finnish housing market are strongly related to the ongoing economic restructuring and its spatial articulation. This is indicated in the migration to centres of growth, which further increased differences between regions. Migration to these centres raised the demand for housing as the economy went through a structural change when new work places were concentrated in a few centres (such as Helsinki, Turku, Tampere, Oulu, Kuopio and Jyväskylä). Between 1996 and 2000, the prices of old dwellings increased by 63% in the capital region, and by 39% in other parts of the country. In 2000, rents in the metropolitan areas were at least 40% higher than the national average. As a consequence, analysts now predict that the number of homeless people might rise, especially within these centres, due to the current difficulties in the rental housing market (Kärkkäinen, 2001).

Ireland

The economic boom of the last decade has contributed to escalating inequalities in income. Higher construction costs and the steep rise in purchasing power among specific sections of the population produced a steep rise in house prices putting owner-occupation beyond the reach of those on an average income (O'Sullivan, 2001). Consequently, access to good quality and affordable housing is now out of the reach of substantial sectors of the Irish population and the pressure on the already overstretched social housing sector has been increased considerably. The primary solution advocated by virtually each analyst of the Irish housing market has been to increase the supply of housing. Indeed, despite an increased supply of new houses during the last decade, mainly geared for the private market sector, Ireland still has a very low number of housing units per 100,000 inhabitants (about 32,000), compared to other member states of the EU (Portugal, Spain, Sweden, Finland and France have more than 47,000 units per 100,000 inhabitants). Furthermore, the geographical distribution of new houses is uneven. A lot of new housing has been concentrated in the private, owner-occupied sector and much of this in recent years has been located in areas other than the primary growth region around Dublin and the east coast. Dublin's share of new additions to the total housing stock declined from 22% in 1995 to just over 12% in 1999. Consequently, housing shortages and house price inflation are more severe in Dublin than elsewhere.

Belgium

The differentiation in Belgian housing prices – and the related pattern of regional housing markets – can be summarised, though perhaps simplistically, by referring to three major features (De Decker, 2001):

• the weight and the influence of the Brussels Capital Region, being the economic core of the country;
• housing quality;
• the fact that Flanders is wealthier than Wallonia.

Consequently, regional differences in dwelling prices and prices of plots of land are substantial. In the cheapest region, (the Mons region in Wallonia), an average middle-sized dwelling costs €48,414, while prices for the same category of dwellings rise to €121,468 in the residential area of Nivelles, south of Brussels. Differences in prices for plots of land are particularly notable: €8.50 in the

Bastogne region (Wallonia), €85 in the Flemish coastal region of Veurne and even €163.20 in the Brussels-Capital Region.

These three examples, and similar development elsewhere, demonstrate that especially affluent and economic centres of growth are characterised by overheated housing markets. However, the inertia of historical housing patterns and traditions also illustrate that these findings cannot be exclusively linked to current trends of globalisation and the flexible investment pattern of international capital. Whatever the balance between current and historically embedded factors might be, it is important to stress that the spread and reproduction of homelessness goes hand in hand with such national patterns of regional housing markets. Indeed, the most overheated regional housing markets also coincide with the most marginalised households being attracted to the informal labour market. These marginalised households are sheltered in the regulated sector of services for the homeless or in informally organised, low-quality segments of the housing market (mattress rental, for example). As such, a large informal housing and labour market, providing the so-called 'underclass' with some basic means of existence, coincides with a generally overheated housing market which is most inaccessible to them and, to a growing extent, even to those with middle class incomes. To put it simply, this boils down to the establishment of deeply polarised European cities in which the homeless are structurally embedded. These polarised cities indeed offer the largest survival infrastructure, ranging from an individually rented bed to a one-week job in the construction or cleaning sector amid the booming economy.

Growing home ownership and the commodification of social housing

The new cycle of growth in the economy, based on the social, economic and spatial principles as described above, is one of the key factors that enabled increases in home ownership in most of the European countries since the 1980s. Although variations occur among the different member states, in relation to the mix of housing tenure and its historically embedded transitions (see Chapter One, Table 1.1), the increase in home ownership in general was encouraged by direct or indirect promotion of subsidies and by the ready availability of mortgages. Therefore, for those who could afford it and who took advantage of the economic growth, home ownership became, at first sight, a valuable alternative to poor quality housing and increasing rents in the private rental market (Van der Heijden and Boelhouwer, 1996). However, several periods of decreased economic growth, going hand in hand with job insecurity and dismissals, left many households, who had only recently become owner-occupiers, with an extensive burden of mortgages and substantial debts. Moreover, at the same time many private landlords were not able to improve the quality of their dwellings, while an ongoing inflation led towards increasing rents, which in turn became a serious problem for tenants.

In the current context of increased home ownership, we want to make a distinction between countries with a long tradition of owner-occupation and countries where this trend has only recently become apparent.

Some countries do have a strong tradition of home ownership. Mediterranean countries are generally in this category. Here, weak formative welfare states provided hardly any social housing in the rental market. In Italy for instance, 69% of the households lived in their own house in 1996 (Tosi, 2001). In Spain, only 14.9% of family housing was rented in 1991 (Cabrera, 2001). However, the large home ownership section of the market is not limited to the Mediterranean part of the EU. In Belgium, Luxembourg and Ireland the housing stock is dominated by home ownership, with two thirds of the stock being owner-occupied. Although these countries – along with Italy, Spain and Portugal – have a strong Catholic tradition, this is not a sufficient grounds for explanation. In the case of the majority of the southern European countries (including Orthodox Greece) the lack of a meaningful social component to their housing stock represents an inheritance of dictatorial regimes ruling for several decades after the Second World War (see for instance Bruto da Costa and Baptista, 2001).

However, in Belgium, since the late 19th century, the Catholic lobbyists have devoted themselves to increasing home ownership among the working class. Home ownership was seen as a strategic instrument to discipline employees in relation to their employers. By giving them the responsibility to take care of their own dwelling, it was thought that strikes or other disturbances would be reduced, since these would hinder the chances of repaying their mortgages. The social consequences of this policy are striking, as De Decker has shown (2001, 2002a). Particularly since the Second World War, the Belgian state has encouraged home ownership through a tax deduction scheme, in the form of a universally accessible grant for all households who enter into a mortgage. In the case of Flanders, De Decker has calculated that in the mid-1990s, more than one million Flemish households profited from approximately €1.5 billion of tax reductions once they became a home-owner (De Decker, 2001). Assuming that owners benefited from these tax deductions in proportion to their income, De Decker observes that only 13% of all benefit from tax deductions goes to the lowest income quintile, while 51% of all benefit from tax deductions goes to the highest income quintile. This is quite a different picture than might have been expected from what is called 'a *social* policy'. Effectively, these findings indicate a substantial difference between rich and poor, demonstrating that the government's initiatives to promote access to private home ownership disadvantages the poorest households.

Access to housing through the private market is increasingly promoted in countries with a less pronounced tradition of home ownership, although there are several contributory factors, the fiscal crisis of the state is one of the more important. The severe crisis of the 1970s and early 1980s reduced public income and urged the state to spend more money on supplementing incomes and other social issues. As a consequence of this situation, public authorities started to market and decentralise some of their key tasks. This process, which can be captured by the change from government to governance (see also Chapter Four of this volume), entailed, for instance, the increasing mediation of both job seeking and low-income housing by private actors and/or lower public authorities. Although this process might reduce bureaucracy and possibly decrease a growing dependency culture on state redistribution, one should not forget that democratic control is also reduced (Imrie and Raco, 1999). Additionally, it is important to note that finding appropriate shelter for the most vulnerable income groups is not a primary concern for the managerial and profit driven forces in the housing market.

Since the late 1970s, then, both the increase of home ownership and the participation of households in the free market are common in European countries with a long tradition of supplying housing to the poorest groups in society. 'Right to buy' has become a general concept that enables sitting tenants in the social rental sector to purchase their dwelling. At the same time, many hundreds of thousands of such dwellings have been transferred to the free market. Partly as a result of the right to buy, the proportion of the owner-occupier housing across the UK is now approximately 68%, with the highest level – 72% – in Wales (Aldridge, 2001). Similarly, the right to buy in Scotland alone has seen the number of social rented houses decline by 34% between 1979 and 1999, with over 400,000 properties sold off. In Wales 110,000 properties were sold off in the same period, and 1.6 million homes in the UK as a whole.

Although the Scandinavian countries in general show some reserve vis-à-vis this general trend towards home ownership, the case of Copenhagen demonstrates that the commodification of public dwellings is no longer taboo in this part of the EU. In order to improve the tax base in the region, the country's capital city was required by the national government to sell a large share of state-owned dwellings, and since 1993, 7% (19,300) of the municipally owned dwellings have been on the free market. The tenants themselves bought about 90% of the dwellings (Nordgaard and Koch-Nielsen, 2001, p 40). In Sweden, many of the municipalities changed their way of using their Municipal Housing Companies (MHCs). This was due to the economic crisis in the first half of the 1990s and to a general ideological change (involving the idea that housing should be market-controlled and that homelessness and risky tenants should be taken care of by the social authorities). The result was that many municipalities reformulated their aims with these companies from social to economic goals. However, because of the Swedish system of rent control the MHC could not be run for profit. As a consequence, both private landlords and MHCs have sold their dwellings and continue to sell their rental buildings to TOSs because it is profitable for them (Sahlin, 2001). A TOS (*bostadsrättsförening*) is a type of economic association that owns a building, and whose members are residents of that building. They pay a monthly fee to cover heating, exterior maintenance, management, and the association's costs for interest, the mortgage and future repairs. Like rental flats, the great majority of these buildings are multi-family houses. The right to dispose of a certain flat is sold on the market to the highest bidder. A conversion of former municipal dwellings to a TOS arrangement has several implications for the access to housing. For instance, relationships among dwellers may change, as some will stay tenants because they are not able to buy and their neighbours, who joined TOS, will become their landlords. Another consequence involves the reduction in rental accommodation, especially in inner cities, with a possible residualisation of the remaining public accommodation. Within a TOS building and even the larger area dominated by this tenure structure, gentrification may increase as first owners move out, selling their dwelling at high prices to more affluent households. Last, competition for remaining rental properties will push up prices, so that selling to TOSs may be part of a process which leads to the establishment of private market rent prices in rental property. Selling rental MHC dwellings to private companies has also occurred in eight municipalities, especially in the wealthy suburbs of Stockholm where the majority of the dwellings remained in the private rental sector. The city itself has decided to offer all MHC flats to the tenants, but only those houses that are attractive (and presumed to be profitable) and which are occupied by sufficiently wealthy tenants, have been sold or will be sold. Residualisation may therefore be a very possible result. More generally, analysts fear that if these trends continue in Sweden, the public sector may disappear and that rents may escalate more widely (Sahlin, 2001).

In Austria, the right to buy by tenants has only been recently introduced by the new government. Schoibl (2001) refers to real estate and other experts who claim that when this process finishes it could mean the complete abolition of all social access and social pricing criteria for rental properties, which, so far, have been publicly supported. A general increase is also expected in housing prices as a long-term consequence of the lack of accommodation that falls within pricing regulations. Principally, however, if the changes are enacted, between 100,000 and 300,000 apartments could suddenly come onto the market and be turned into private property. The exact number of properties to be privatised will depend on not only whether housing associations in public ownership sell off their properties, but also whether housing development agencies owned by banks, funds and insurance companies can shed their obligation to provide housing for the 'common good'. Furthermore, it will depend on the Austrian counties and cities if this transformation of the 'common good' status will also affect associations at the regional or city council levels.

Increases in home ownership are also present in the housing market in the Netherlands. Although the coalition agreement of 1978 emphasised home ownership in the Netherlands, it was only successfully promoted by a town planning policy document (the so-called VINEX) in 1997. This means that in specially designated areas, home ownership is promoted by the central government. The share of home ownership rose significantly between 1956 and 1996, from 29% to 48% (Boelhouwer, 2000). However, a breakdown by household type reveals that almost all households in all income quartiles show rising proportions of home ownership, except for single-person households in the lowest income category (De Feijter, 2001, p 13). In Greece, home ownership also tends to follow the income pattern but with some remarkable exceptions. For example, there is a marked tendency, as well as capability, for households to move into home ownership as they get older. The rate of home ownership has increased by 25-30% in such households (Maloutas, 1990). This is largely due to the fact that economic insecurity has urged Greeks to invest in housing rather than the stock market or other forms of industry. This is usually expressed through people buying their house and often that of their children (Sapounakis, 2001).

However, as Tosi illustrates (2001), the general trend of home ownership is also present among the poorer classes in Italy. This phenomenon is generally known as 'enforced' home ownership and it has developed all over Europe. Dramatic rises in rent prices in the private market combined with a cutback in the social housing supply persuaded many low-income households to buy their own dwelling. The limited purchasing power gives them access only to the poorest housing, with dwellings often lacking even the most basic amenities. This frequently goes hand in hand with insecure housing conditions, which are linked to unpredictable changes in land use and other problems. In general, home ownership has increased in Italy due to a combination of various factors, such as laws to assist purchase, and high levels of inflation that reduced long-term debt. This has meant that home ownership is present across different classes in Italy. However, as Tosi writes, the most significant 'welfare' consequence of the extension of home ownership is the existence of poor owners. This can be exemplified with the case of Lombardy, one of the richest regions in the country, where the home ownership rate is at nearly 70%, but where 40% of households below the poverty threshold also own their homes. A substantial proportion of the poorer population had to purchase, especially in recent years, housing in badly served urban areas or housing that is in a generally bad condition. Limited purchasing power frequently made it impossible to meet the cost of repairs or essential improvements to the house.

In the UK, research by the Council of Mortgage Lenders (CML) revealed that low-income home owners live in dwellings in need of modernisation and lacking amenities (Council of Mortgage Lenders, 2000). The estimated costs of urgent repairs for home-owner households in the lowest income quintile in 1996 was £2.8 billion (€4.5 billion). This research also revealed that the growth of low-income households within the home-owner sector cannot be solely attributed to the direct entry of low-income households into the sector. Rather, it is the result of changes of circumstances (unemployment, ill health, relationship breakdown or retirement) that reduce incomes of previously better-off households.

In Portugal, low-income households are caught between high prices in the private housing market (rental prices, soil prices, and so on), lack of private renting alternatives and the lack of social housing. They are therefore forced either to buy their own houses or to remain excluded from the formal housing market, obliged to live in insecure housing conditions (Bruto da Costa and Baptista, 2001, p 9). The same trend can be observed in Belgium where the low level of production of new houses creates a large stock of old and badly equipped houses. Combined with steep rises in prices in the private market and a lack of sufficient social housing, many low-budget households are forced to purchase in this section of the market, in rural as well as in urban areas. In the deprived areas of larger cities, Turks in particular have owned their dwellings during the 1980s and 1990s (Kesteloot et al, 1998). Many of them look for additional incomes by renting rooms; this pays for basic maintenance or to refund mortgages. A relatively high proportion of these rooms is rented by relatives and friends (Meert, 1998; De Decker, 2001; Meert et al, 2002b). At the same time, such strategies go hand in hand with overcrowded housing conditions. Overcrowding of privately owned dwellings in the free market is a common problem. This type of inadequate housing is reported by many European member states, for example in the Portuguese case where, in the early 1990s, 13% of the families were living in overcrowded lodging (Bruto da Costa and Baptista, 2001, p 16).

Deregulation and bifurcation of the private housing market

Deregulation and bifurcation of the private housing market also demonstrate that the impact of the public authority has changed drastically in the field of housing. Although this theme will be elaborated in more detail in Chapter Four, the deregulation of the private housing market is an important trend to discuss here in relation to homelessness. Indeed, this process, taking into account our discussion of the commodification of social housing, reduces the capacity of the state to maintain a permanent safety-net for the weakest income groups. The cutback of certain rules, such as rent control, may reinforce the process of excluding large social groups from access to a decent dwelling as corrupt landlords will be encouraged to offer insecure and substandard accommodation in order to increase their profits.

While the deregulation process of the private housing market is widely spread across the EU, there are some countervailing tendencies. Very recently, for instance, Germany has seen a reform of tenancy law, including the reduction of the limits of possible rent increases and the possibilities of time-limited rent contracts (Busch-Geertsema, 2001). Nevertheless, in many countries both the privately owned sector and the private rental sector have been affected by deregulation.

In the case of home ownership, the deregulation of the housing finance markets has led to a dramatic growth in mortgages and has persuaded many low-income households to purchase their own dwelling. We have noted already that this trend, together with unpredictable periods of slowdown in economic growth, has led to an increased share of households who are unable to pay back their mortgages and who are therefore locked into considerable debt. In the UK the rush to home ownership was in part at least responsible for the high levels of mortgage repossession in the 1990s. In the first half of 1999, while the housing market was supposedly booming, 16,410 households experienced mortgage possession – that is over 630 a week, or over 90 a day. These households join the 454,280 that had already experienced mortgage possession in the 1990s. Over the last decade well over 1.3 million adults and children have lost their homes due to mortgage default.

The ongoing deregulation process in formerly more regulated housing markets is illustrated by recent Austrian policy developments. Here, the recent policy of deregulation and liberalisation has led to a worsening of the access to good housing and the ability of large groups in society to obtain social security (Schoibl, 2001). In the private housing market, more and more low-income households are faced with high costs, short tenancy periods, additional administrative costs by profit oriented estate agencies, and the repeated need to move from one flat to the next. As a consequence, the most deprived segments of the private housing market have become an essential source of housing for low-income households. Moreover, the switch from bricks and mortar to individual subsidies induced a further deterioration of the private housing market. Not only communal development agencies but also eligible individuals could then apply to receive public subsidies and thus could choose any construction provider to 'cash in' the state's obligation. Consequently, the public authorities lost their influence on the development of the housing market as well as on the quality of housing. Social and qualitative aspects of the development of deprived and segregated neighbourhoods were sidelined and have since become increasingly neglected.

A consequence of this deregulation entails the bifurcation of the private housing sector. On the one hand, both the owner and the rental sectors are characterised by higher income households who benefit from economic growth and for which either a long-term ownership or a more flexible formulae of renting a decent and fashionable dwelling fits their needs. It is this group, with their purchasing power, who are acquiring a growing share of the market. On the other hand, enforced home ownership creates within the sector of owner-occupiers a significant proportion of marginalised households. The same occurs within the private rental sector where low-income migrants, asylum seekers, youngsters and other people surviving on a minimum wage or on informal incomes, are sheltered and survive.

Exclusion strategies adopted by landlords clearly contribute to the bifurcation of the private rental sector and the creation of a residual of dwellings, left to the most marginalised people when all other, more decent possibilities have become inaccessible to them. For instance, in the case of Germany, there is a lot of evidence that private landlords discriminate on the basis of nationality (race), age and supposed purchasing power (Busch-Geertsema, 2001), although these practices are not new. Also in Ireland, many private landlords are unwilling to accept 'risky tenants' because of their perceptions of such tenants as less reliable and their preference for a 'better class' of tenant. O' Sullivan refers to research in the city of Cork where of 173 landlords interviewed, almost three quarters said they would not accept rent supplement tenants (O'Sullivan, 2001, p 37).

A more systematic approach to the question of whether there is bifurcation in the private rental market has been presented by De Decker (2001) in his discussion of Belgium. He analysed the official private rental sector, by using several sources of statistical data from 1997 and 1999 on education, professional status and other socio-economic indicators in Flanders and compared it with the social rental sector, non-subsidised and subsidised owner. He concludes that the clearest residualisation occurs in the case of private renting. However, the typical occupant of residualised private rental property is relatively highly educated but with low income. The simplest explanation for this is that private tenants are first time buyers in the private market, who moreover mostly live alone (De Decker, 2001).

Conclusion

The general conclusion of this chapter is that, despite the historically developed regulating dialectic between market exchange, state redistribution and reciprocity, there is a clear trend in the EU of the commodification of housing. This trend has far-reaching consequences, as the ongoing process of privatisation or conversion of public rental flats into owner-occupied ones is almost irreversible. It will not be possible to buy back sold properties at reasonable costs, and it would take centuries to restore the balance through new public construction.

The trend of commodification goes hand in hand with a clear rhetoric that people feel upgraded when they own their homes, that they become more proud and willing to work. More fundamentally, the trend of commodification is embedded in neoliberal economic theory that the market should allocate as much as possible of goods and services and that the state should interfere as little as possible in the free market dynamics. Therefore, it is clear that the new allocation model of housing in general relies on an increasing importance of pure market exchange. Although it is clear that each European country and welfare state regime has its own specificities, four common trends can be identified as characterising this complex process:

- the growing exclusion of the most vulnerable and marginalised group from the labour market and consequently from access to housing;
- the new post-Fordist logic of spatial organisation and the eviction of the weakest players in the urban housing markets;
- the increase of (enforced) home ownership (including the implementation of the right to buy);
- the deregulation and related bifurcation of the private housing market.

Sahlin makes an interesting distinction between 'the market solution' and 'a rights solution'. In sum, for reasons that we also discussed in this chapter and which take account of the private market's place in a broader regulating context, Sahlin (2001) argues that improving access to housing for low-income groups through a strict market solution should also entail some kind of insurance against homelessness. It also has to entail the restriction on other societal markets (such as the interrelated labour market), "in such a way that the resources of 'customers' are levelled and housing needs are expressed and acknowledged as demand for housing". Sahlin continues by arguing that the market solution "should also imply institutions that counteract trust-building, monopolistic or moralistic behaviour among the property owners" (2001, p 84).

Taking into account the former, we subscribe to Sahlin's 'rights solution', which entails the establishment of a general right to housing. In fact, this solution boils down to restoring the central steering capacity of the state. Indeed, housing as a fundamental means of existence cannot be entirely organised by market- and profit-led motivations. The fact that in many European member states housing production substantially decreased when the bricks and mortar subsidies were abolished, proves that the private market is not successful in providing a quantitatively and qualitatively satisfying supply of houses (see for example, De Decker, 2002b; Dewilde and De Keulenaer, 2002). Therefore, to realise the general right to housing within the EU, public control – at least initially – is needed. This will include the identification of housing production targets and forms of tenure in order to secure a sufficient supply of affordable rental housing. Second, such a right would also require public control over the allocation of a reasonable number of rental dwellings, inter alia, to avoid exclusion by private and public landlords (see Chapter Four of this volume) which would hinder the access to decent dwellings for the most vulnerable and marginalised groups.

When we consider this last idea in terms of modes of economic integration, it entails a plea for an adapted regulation regime of the housing market. Perhaps a more powerful intervention using the principles of redistribution is needed. Indeed, as we will argue more extensively in Chapter Five, one should not romanticise too much about including the third sphere of reciprocity. Similarly, market exchange also lacks the capacity to prevent marginalised members of a community from being excluded or exploited (see Chapter Seven for further discussion of these issues).

Notes

[1] This threefold distinction between market exchange, redistribution and reciprocity was introduced in the literature by Karl Polanyi (1944) and has been extensively discussed in numerous contributions and disciplines (see, for example, Harvey [1973]; and Mingione [1991]).

[2] For Paris, see Morokvasic (1987); for Italy, see Quassoli (1999); for Berlin, see Hillmann (1999); for Brussels, see Kesteloot and Meert (1999); for Marseilles, see Péraldi (2000); for London, see Economic Policy Group (nd).

[3] Similar conclusions are made for Brussels in Kesteloot et al (1998); for Belfast in Boal (1998); for Paris in White (1998); for Hamburg in Friederichs (1998).

FOUR

Access to affordable housing

Introduction

This chapter considers the impact of the changing nature of governance in the European housing market on access to housing for low-income and vulnerable groups. The central feature of governance change relates to the 'hollowing out' of state responsibilities, involving both decentralisation and institutional reorganisation in all EU member states. Since the hey-day of state involvement in the provision of housing in the 1960s, the role of the state has shifted from a concern with redistribution of resources to a focus on regulation and risk management. The regulatory role of the state has been shaped principally to accommodate the market and to facilitate an increasing reliance on private finance in the delivery of public services. The process of decentralisation of responsibility, together with an increasing emphasis on individual responsibility (witnessed in the promotion of home ownership) and an increasing reliance on third sector housing providers, compromise the ability of the state to protect the vulnerable and economically weak sections of society in the housing market.

The availability, adequacy and affordability of housing configure the landscape on which the story of accessibility for vulnerable groups is drawn. The changing nature of this landscape in terms of the impact of increasing housing costs on the vulnerability of households in the housing market and on the ability of these households to pay for adequate and decent housing is discussed in section one of this chapter. This is principally in relation to changes in the rental market (private and social), which is contracting and restricting opportunities for access to affordable and adequate housing. The increasing uncertainty and volatility of private housing markets and the declining importance of private rented housing emphasises the pivotal role of social housing in ensuring access to affordable housing for homeless people and vulnerable households. The issues concerned with access to social housing form the basis of the second section of the chapter. The third section of the chapter moves on to consider the nature of support and housing in relation to issues of access to housing for vulnerable groups. It concentrates on the sometimes complex issues relating to the integration of housing policy and welfare policy, and the perceived segmentation of the housing market in relation to allocation and access for vulnerable groups and homeless people generally.

In the face of the declining supply of affordable housing and increasing volatility (or real-price increases) in housing costs in most parts of Europe, why has homelessness not increased more than it has and why, in some countries, has homelessness remained static or even declined? The homeless are not passive victims of socio-political and economic change, and find coping mechanisms within a situation of increasing risk in a volatile housing market. As well as those who are well housed and those who are excluded from the housing market, there is a growing segment of the population at risk of housing exclusion. This chapter concludes by summarising the factors underpinning this risk and provides a framework for Chapter Five, which considers the coping mechanisms of these vulnerable households.

Changing governance of housing

The role of the state in the housing market has been changing in Europe over the last twenty years. While it is difficult to generalise across all welfare regimes about the nature of this change, or the factors that underpin it, there are nevertheless some common strands in evidence. Within countries,

> ... there has been a shift throughout the 1980s to expand sub-national and municipal competencies in housing both in countries with historically strong housing policies, such as Denmark and France, and those developing a new emphasis in housing policy, such as Spain and Ireland. (MacLennan et al, 1996, p 1)

Changes in financing of housing production, deregulation of financial markets and moves towards monetary union have had an impact on national housing policies in general and social housing policy in particular (Priemus and Dieleman, 1999). Housing policy has also been influenced by integrated approaches to urban and community regeneration and therefore is influenced by social, urban and environmental policies (Skifter-Andersen, 1999). Important common themes in policy development have been described by a number of authors (MacLennan et al, 1996; Kleinman, 1998; Priemus and Dieleman, 1999; Gibb, 2002) to include:

- a greater role for markets in the production, allocation and financing of housing;
- the promotion of home ownership;
- the decline in the social housing sector;
- deregulation of housing finance markets;
- a switch from property subsidies to housing allowances;
- a decline in public expenditure on housing;
- a switch from new building to renovation;
- greater market orientation and private sector ethos of social housing agencies;
- targeting of social housing subsidies.

Priemus and Dieleman (1999) chart the broad changes in housing policy in Europe from the heady days of the welfare state in the 1950s/1960s when many governments began to provide social housing in the face of persistent housing shortages and scarcity of investment capital. At this time public loans were commonplace and constituted a hidden property subsidy. The shift away from public loans combined with decentralisation of decision making led to the introduction of housing allowances to cushion the impact of increasing rents on household budgets. Gradually during the 1970s and 1980s policies of deregulation of rents, reduction in property subsidies and a more vigorous promotion of home ownership were adopted. Everywhere in western Europe housing and housing finance systems became more market-oriented. Since the 1980s housing expenditure has declined as a share of the national budget and private housing outlays increased in almost every country as restraints were imposed on public spending. Almost everywhere the production of new social rented housing has been declining consistently since the early 1980s.

These policy themes have emerged in the context of a crisis of the welfare state that has witnessed a 'hollowing out' of the state as governments of all political colours have grappled with the burgeoning costs of public services. This hollowing out refers to the shift of responsibilities to supra-national structures (for example, EU competencies) and a parallel shift of functions downwards to regional and local levels. This shift is associated with the reorganisation of the local state as "new forms of local partnership emerge to guide and promote the development of local resources" (Jessop, 1994, p 264). An optimistic scenario of this process envisages strong regional economies providing reciprocal support to retain a competitive edge (Sabel, 1989). More pessimistic scenarios anticipate "growing polarisation within localities (including the rise of an urban underclass and inner city ghettoes) as well as increased regional inequalities" (Jessop, 1994, p 264). One effect of this shift towards the regional or local level is a growing variety of forms and strategies of intervention and increasing use of public-private partnership structures. One implication of this shift is that, while the central state provides resources and guidance, increasingly innovation in service level provision and supply-side structures occurs at the local level and is reliant on strong local networks (see Edgar et al, 1999).

This changing role of the state in housing policy has developed at a time when it has been perceived that crude housing shortages have largely ended and the housing problem is now conceptualised as one of local imbalances and of sectional and special needs issues. Although such perceptions underpin changes in housing policy, our analysis demonstrates a re-emergence of shortages of affordable social housing, a re-establishment of the link between poverty and poor housing and an increasing segment of households at risk of homelessness or living in precarious housing circumstances.

Hence, in the context of this study, the change in the governance of housing is reflected in three interrelated trends:

1. the decentralisation of responsibilities from central government to regional and municipal tiers of government and within this shift the changing role of local government to 'enabling' authorities;

2. reflecting the enabling role of government, the move to non-governmental institutional structures to meet social housing objectives;
3. a decreasing political priority for (social) housing which is reflected in a shift towards 'weakly regulated market structures' (Ball and Harloe, 1998) and a greater reliance on private finance to meet social housing objectives.

A fourth trend may be tentatively suggested which reflects the historically weak welfare role of housing in the development of social welfare regimes in Europe. During the last decade, the development of 'care in the community' policies associated with de-institutionalisation, at least in northern European countries (see Edgar et al, 2000), has led to the emergence of new funding and regulatory mechanisms of government to 'support people' in housing in the community. This has been associated with new institutional structures, emerging forms of inter-agency working and new municipal models of commissioning housing and support. This increased integration of housing and social welfare objectives (albeit embryonic) may reflect new models of social housing provision and governance.

Some authors have argued that the decentralisation of housing policy reflects a weakening policy priority for housing, in the context of the ending of crude housing shortages, leading to an overwhelming policy preference for a "private, weakly regulated market framework" (Ball and Harloe, 1998, p 60). Kleinman (1998), on the other hand, argues for a collapse in housing policy that is manifest in a bifurcation of policy issues. One set of concerns, he argues, relates to the circumstances of the majority that is mainly well housed. Housing outcomes for this group are affected by government interventions, which ensure continuity and reasonable market conditions in the private sector. The second set of concerns relate to the circumstances of the most disadvantaged and vulnerable who are badly housed or homeless and whose prospects for future betterment are uncertain. Whichever perspective is preferred, the effect of this retrenchment in government intervention remains: in the changing locus of decision making, in the changing institutional framework of decisions and in the impact of a more market-oriented framework of finance on access to housing.

Decentralisation of responsibilities

The decentralisation of decision making in housing policy to the regional and municipal tiers of government has led to an increasing diversity in housing systems and a suggestion of widening inequalities in the face of differential regional economic competitiveness. The case of Austria illustrates the effects of such decentralisation, where the legislative and administrative competence for housing policy shifted from the federal government to the regional authorities in 1988. The shift from federal to regional authority also occurred in other federal countries such as Belgium (during the 1970s). In Austria, this shift has been associated with the introduction of public subsidies to private building firms and plans to 'liberalise' the social housing market selling up to 300,000 dwellings to private investment funds, banks and insurance companies. This is occurring at a time of increasing localised housing shortages in the regional capitals. On the positive side, some counties and city governments have responded with small-scale local initiatives such as the 'easy access initiative' for vulnerable and disadvantaged families organised by the communal housing agency in Vienna.

Recent changes in housing governance in Italy will have implications for access to housing for homeless and vulnerable groups. The present situation is still 'working itself out' and the impact of these changes are not at all clear at present. As with many other countries in Europe, Italy has decentralised the responsibility for housing. Over the past decade financial provision and planning responsibilities have been gradually devolved to the regions and the municipalities, including responsibility for the politically sensitive process of selecting applicants for social housing. These changes have disrupted and weaken the traditional role and responsibilities of the Autonomous Institutes for Social Housing (IACPs). At present the precise roles of these respective agencies in relation to provision, allocation and management of social housing are not fully worked out and, furthermore, demonstrate marked regional differences. In a further complication, voluntary agencies, which have always had a strong presence in relation to other welfare services in Italy are now being drawn into housing provision, setting up a rival 'third sector'. As Tosi (2001) comments, the resolution to the search for a 'local operator' will determine the extent to which public and/or private agencies will be involved in the delivery of rental housing. The outcome will have implications for the accessibility of housing for homeless and vulnerable groups throughout Italy, which has one of the lowest levels of privately and socially rented housing in Europe.

Institutional structure of social housing

The institutional structure of the social rented sector is diverse and has been changing in most countries (Priemus and Boelhouwer, 1999). Gibb (2002) identifies three main structures by which the processes of provision, financing, management and regulation of social housing are implemented. These structures include municipal provision (for example, the UK and Austria), municipal companies (for example, Sweden) and private or voluntary non-profit housing associations (for example, the Netherlands, Denmark and Germany). The French *habitations à loyers modérés* (HLM) are moderate rent properties owned by public organisations sponsored by local authorities which, as non-profit agencies, are similar to housing associations. Gibb's description ignores the fact that in Germany social rented dwellings may be operated by private parties seeking to make a profit as well as by non-profit organisations (Priemus and Boelhouwer, 1999; Busch-Geertsema, 2001). Cooperative housing (for example, Finland, Denmark and Sweden) provides a hybrid example of social housing provision.

The changing institutional structures of the social housing sector arise for different reasons that have distinct implications for access to affordable housing for vulnerable groups. Several countries have a very small social rented sector including Spain, Portugal, Greece, Belgium, Luxembourg, Italy and Ireland. Some of these countries (Spain, Ireland and Portugal) have adopted policies to increase the supply of social housing. Greece has no social housing owned and managed by statutory bodies and policies continue to promote the growth of home ownership through public subsidies. In those countries with a substantial social housing sector the main change in institutional structures has been the shift from municipal provision to the not-for-profit sector (MacLennan et al, 1996; Priemus and Dieleman, 1999). This shift has been associated with the move towards more market-oriented housing finance systems (Priemus and Dieleman, 1999).

The decline in investment in social housing together with subsidised sales policies has led to a significant contraction in the social housing sector in the UK and Ireland. MacLennan et al (1996) suggest that some countries continued a strong commitment to social housing investment during the 1980s, including the Netherlands, Sweden, France, Austria and Germany. During the 1990s the relative decline in the sector has become apparent in Sweden and the Netherlands and more recently budgets have declined in Denmark and France. Only Ireland, Portugal and Germany have given new priority to social housing in the late 1990s. Priemus and Dieleman (1999) argue that the decline in the provision of new social rented dwellings is likely to continue in the coming years.

In Austria and Germany the original subsidy arrangements under which social housing was provided are reaching the end of their lifespan, and the sector is declining and the ownership profile changing as a result. According to Busch-Geertsema (2001), West German housing policy in the postwar period aimed at applying the principles of the German social market economy to the housing sector. The mechanisms used were planned to be time-limited and as such social obligations for state subsidised social housing were also time-limited. The direct provision and ownership of housing by municipalities was, largely, avoided and private as well as capital-oriented investors were accepted and funded as social landlords. The term 'social housing' therefore describes a method of financing housing together with a set of regulations and responsibilities about allocation of tenancies, rent levels and standards, rather than a physically identifiable stock of dwellings (Kleinman, 1996). Busch-Geertsema (2001) quotes unpublished statistics which indicate that, between 1950 and 1999, 8.6 million social housing units were subsidised in West Germany (under various support schemes as indicated in the 2nd Housing Construction Law). Of these, approximately 3.2 million were social housing units for owner-occupiers and about 5.4 million were social rented flats. Only 2.3 million social rented housing units remained in 1999. Therefore, for more than half of the rental social housing units which were subsidised social obligations have now run out and the dwellings have reverted to the status of private housing. This process will continue and it is assumed that only one million social rental housing dwellings will be left in Germany in 2005 (GDW, 1998, p 23).

This reduction in the scale of social housing in Germany is now to be accompanied by a major change in housing policy. Hitherto subsidies for social housing have been aimed at the broad strata of society rather than being targeted to disadvantaged groups. The income ceilings set for allocation of social housing were, for much of the postwar period, set high enough to include the majority of the population. The legal situation changes in 2002 when a new act – called *Wohnraumförderungsgesetz* (WoFG) – will replace the aim of state support for the housing needs of "broad strata of the population" by specifying that the target group is "households which are not able to procure decent housing by themselves and are in need of support" (s 1). Groups specifically mentioned include pregnant women, large families, single parents, the elderly and severely disabled people and "households with low incomes". Explicit reference is made to "homeless persons and other persons in need of support" (BMVBW, 2001a, p 34). Persons in need of support are defined as households threatened by homelessness and households living in unacceptable housing conditions. Therefore it can be said that German housing policy is at a turning point from a universal approach towards more targeted measures. The states (*Bundesländer*) and the municipalities will get more freedom to decide on details of their housing policy, but they will also get less funding for it from central government.

Changing financial systems have been instrumental in changing the institutional structure of social housing provision especially in countries where housing associations are key social landlords (the Netherlands, UK, Denmark, Germany). In the UK, restrictions on public sector borrowing by local authorities has led, over recent years, to an increasing trend to transfer council housing stock to housing association ownership. The scale of these transfers is projected to increase in future years. Priemus and Dieleman comment on the impact, on the institutional structure of social landlords, of the "shift from public loans to private loans, from interest subsidies to market interest rates and from property subsidies to housing allowances" (1999, p 630). The shift to a greater reliance on private sector finance has meant that social landlords have had "to rethink their strategies and minimise their risk while becoming more commercial and cost-effective" (Pryke and Whitehead, 1995, p 630). The most direct impact of market rates of finance has been higher rents. Risk minimisation has been associated with policies to guarantee the rental stream – allocation policies favouring less risky tenants, a more stringent approach to evictions and the management of vacancies. Priemus and Dieleman also suggest that social landlords have been restructuring and repositioning in the market reflected in a greater reluctance, by some housing associations, to take the risks associated with development on brownfield and inner city sites. This is increasingly seen to be incompatible with the social purpose of housing associations meeting the needs of the most vulnerable in the housing market. In a private finance market, size and economies of scale also become issues in guaranteeing debt and long run maintenance. Larger associations and greater financial control tend to conflict with objectives of tenant participation and management. In this context the governance of social housing and its financial accountability is a major issue. Gibb suggests that "local government will play a key role, either supervising social landlords or enabling them strategically, for instance through the land market or financial guarantees" (2002, p 333). In this case the hollowing out of the state, following the deregulation of financial markets, is manifest in an increased role for regulation to guarantee accountability and risk management among social landlords.

In some countries strong economic growth or an overheating in the metropolitan housing market has led to significant changes in the institutional structure of social housing provision. In Ireland, an economic boom led to rapidly rising house prices especially in the Dublin region and a recognition that home ownership was out of the reach of substantial sectors of the population. Plans for social housing provision (in 1991 and 1995) have increased output and led to a 'second coming' for voluntary sector housing associations in Ireland (O'Sullivan, 2001). The Minister for the Environment has established a specific Voluntary and Cooperative Housing Unit in the department to develop the role of the sector. Finland is perhaps unique in the EU in that the share of owner-occupation in the stock fell significantly during the 1990s. This followed an intense speculative boom in the late 1980s which was followed by an equally dramatic fall in prices leading to mortgage defaults and tighter lending restrictions while new entrants were put off by falling real prices. As a result government policy aimed to encourage the revival of the rental sector and introduced a hybrid ownership-rental tenure – the 'right of occupancy' dwelling modelled on the Swedish tenant ownership cooperatives.

In Portugal, EU-funded programmes for urban regeneration (the PER) have been influential in changing social housing structures. The growth of public housing in Portugal has been slow, irregular and concentrated in Lisbon and Porto. The PER and cooperation agreements marked the final transfer of responsibility for the promotion of public housing from central government to local authorities. This was accomplished by means of protocols that associated financial support for municipalities to total transfer of public housing stock to the municipalities of Lisbon and Porto. In the PER private enterprises built houses on municipal land and then sold them to the municipalities at prices regulated by the state.

Affordable housing

Whether homelessness is viewed primarily as a housing problem or as a social welfare problem (Vranken, 1995; Tosi, 2001), it is clear that accommodation and financial support are two of the main needs of vulnerable and homeless people to which public policy must respond. This section provides the context for the examination of these issues of housing supply and housing subsidy. The context for this examination is well summarised in the EU communication on the first National Action Plans for Social Inclusion (NAPs/incl) submitted in June 2001:

When it comes to low-income sections of the population however the (housing) market is performing less satisfactorily in most Member States and increasingly so. The declining supply of reasonably priced houses at the lower end of the housing market tends to push a rising number of households without adequate purchasing power into the residual segment of the market. (European Commission, 2001, p 36)

Access to decent housing for vulnerable and low-income groups depends on an adequate supply of affordable housing. Historically, governments have intervened in the housing market to break the link between poverty and poor housing when this was perceived to be damaging to social or political stability or economic competitiveness (Malpass and Murie, 1997). This intervention took several forms including state provision of housing, income protection and subsidy to housing consumption. Recent changes in the housing market in Europe would suggest that this link between low income and poor housing is being re-established (Ball and Harloe, 1998). The high cost of housing can itself create poverty even where government assistance to housing costs is available. This occurs when net housing costs are at a level that leaves households with a net residual income that is below the poverty threshold. Equally, the lack of reasonably priced and accessible housing constrains the coping strategies of people who do not have family support, of households at transition points in their life course and of households coping with crisis or relationship breakdown.

The EU strategy to combat poverty and social exclusion has the objective to ensure access for all to decent and sanitary housing at a price they can afford. The meaning of affordability in relation to housing presents difficulties both conceptually and operationally. The conceptual difficulty resides in the need to establish a normative definition of the housing good and what households should pay for that good. The normative definition of adequate or decent housing determines the nature of affordability and yet this is a vague and relative concept. Since 1950 the proportion of income spent on housing has risen, for all households, as real incomes have risen. What proportion of income should we expect households, at different income levels, to pay for housing? The operational difficulty in defining affordability lies in the measurement of housing costs and the extent to which social assistance and housing allowances are treated as housing support or income support.

If the definition of adequate, decent and sanitary housing can be determined, then a simple definition of affordability is that the price of that unit of accommodation (net of state subsidy) is "not an unreasonable burden on household income" (MacLennan and Williams, 1990, p 15). To understand the implications of this simple definition for vulnerable or low-income households it is necessary to consider the household income and expenditure. The household has a net income (that is, net of tax), from which a range of items of expenditure must be met. Household expenditure includes:

- direct housing costs (mortgage or rent, house maintenance);
- housing-related costs (insurance, tax, utilities);
- transport costs (location of housing related to employment);
- other goods and services;
- debt repayment;
- savings (and, in the case of immigrants, remittances sent home).

The nature of expenditure will vary depending on whether the household owns the dwelling outright, owns with a mortgage or rents from a public or private landlord. In order to consider the relationship between household income and expenditure we may consider the broad elements of household expenditure, irrespective of tenure, to meet the costs of a unit of 'adequate, decent and sanitary' housing. A satisfactory position is achieved when household income is high enough to meet housing costs as well as the consumption of other goods and services. An 'unsatisfactory' situation is reached, it is suggested, in three scenarios in relation to housing affordability (Oxley and Smith, 1996).

In the first scenario, household income is too low to meet the costs of the minimum housing standard. The implications of this scenario for the state are to raise incomes (generally or selectively) or to influence the price of housing (generally or selectively, object subsidies) or to reduce expenditure on housing (subject subsidies). The implications for the household may be reliance on family, social networks or reciprocal relationships, reliance on service providers or 'confessional' support, or homelessness (rooflessness). Since the household income is so low it is not an option for the household to reduce consumption of other goods and services. However, for many households in this situation one coping strategy is often to resort to (informal) loans and high levels of indebtedness.

In the second scenario, residual income after paying (net) housing costs results in poverty. The implications for the state remain to raise incomes selectively by targeted housing subsidies or by income support to achieve an acceptable affordability threshold defined in terms of the state poverty threshold. The implications for the household revolve around a reduction in consumption of other goods and services, repayments and savings. In this scenario the household consumption of the minimum standard of housing is met.

In the third scenario, the household's residual income after paying (net) non-housing costs results in housing poverty. In this scenario, the household has achieved a consumption of other goods and services to meet its (minimal) needs. The implication of this scenario for the family is the reduction in housing consumption (below the defined decent and sanitary housing standard).

This consideration of housing affordability emphasises the interrelatedness of the factors involved. On the one hand, public policies related to housing and social protection systems affect the situation of different types of household. The tenure structure and housing opportunities in the housing market will affect the ability of households to adjust their consumption patterns. Furthermore, the household's decision making and choices, at different stages in the life course, will reflect their relative priorities and ability to pay for consumption of housing and other goods and services and the trade-offs they are prepared to make in relation to housing and non-housing costs in order to cope. This choice-based consideration assumes, of course, that the household has the information to enable it to make decisions about competing alternatives.

Access to affordable housing is in large measure dependent on the tenure structure of the housing market. (The implications, for vulnerable households, of the growth of home ownership for access to housing are discussed in Chapter Three of this volume.) Government responses to the dilemma of encouraging home ownership and facilitating access to affordable housing for the most vulnerable differs across the four European welfare regimes. In Ireland, the response has been to establish a commission of inquiry into house prices (Bacon, 2000) and to promote, in the Planning and Development Act 2000, an increased provision of social rented housing. In Belgium, the establishment of social rental agencies has aimed to ease access to the private rented sector. In Finland, the creation of a new 'right of occupancy' tenure in 1990 has facilitated access to housing for young and new families who can not afford home ownership prices. In Italy, recent legislation has focussed on affordable rent control and introduced rent allowances as a general measure for low-income households. On the other hand, the Greek NAP/incl suggests that "despite the high rates of owner-occupation, the promotion of home ownership for low-income individuals remains a basic objective of government" (Sapounakis, 2001, p 29).

This analysis therefore predicates that access to adequate housing is dependent on the supply of accessible and affordable rented housing in which households have security of tenure. A number of key features are evident across Europe in relation to the ability of the rental sector to meet the needs of vulnerable households for affordable accommodation. First, in most parts of Europe the rental sector overall (and the social housing sector in some countries) is in decline. Second, the rental sector is highly segmented (both functionally and spatially). Third, the costs of rental housing are increasing relative to income. Fourth, housing allowances are effective in reducing housing costs but, nevertheless, the proportion of income devoted to housing is highest for those on lowest incomes. One implication of these trends in influencing the availability of affordable housing is to emphasise the importance of social housing in facilitating access to decent housing for vulnerable groups.

Decline in rental housing

The ability of vulnerable households to access affordable rented housing is clearly compromised where the rented sector is small or is declining. Taken as a whole (including public and private rented housing), there has been a long-running decline in the amount of rented housing in all EU member states since at least the 1960s. Although it is often convenient to make a distinction between private and social rented housing, as we have commented earlier the difference between these two categories is blurred in several European countries.

In these circumstances tenure categories defined by who owns the housing are less important than considerations of how the housing is allocated and how rents are set (Oxley, 1995). Within the context of a long-running decline, the impact of the shifting balance between social and private rented accommodation and the impact on vulnerable households will vary from country to country, reflecting differences in allocation mechanisms, rent levels and security of tenure.

The different forms of provision and ownership of rented housing were discussed earlier in this chapter. It has also been shown (Table 1.1) that six countries (Spain, Italy, Greece, Portugal, Ireland and Finland) have relatively small rented housing sectors well below the EU average of 37%. In the Mediterranean countries the vast majority of this housing is privately provided. In Belgium and Luxembourg, similarly, the majority of rented accommodation is in private ownership and social rented housing is insignificant. Germany, with the highest proportion of rented accommodation in Europe, has a more mixed ownership structure, but here too most rented accommodation is privately owned (although a proportion of this is subsidised for allocation under social housing criteria). Elsewhere the rental sector is broadly evenly split between private and social rented housing.

Even in the Mediterranean countries, with some of the lowest levels of rental accommodation in Europe, the rental sector has been declining over the long run, especially since the 1980s. In Spain, the rental sector declined from 51% of the housing stock in 1950 to 15% in 1999. It has been argued that "Spain not only has the lowest supply of rented houses, but it has the highest rate of individually owned property, the lowest rate of public rented accommodation and the highest rate of loss of this system of assignment of accommodation in Europe" (Paniagua, 1995, p 60). In Portugal the rented sector (overall) declined from 43% of the housing stock in 1981 to 29% in 1998, although the social rented sector increased from 7% to 13% in the same period. The rented sector in Italy declined dramatically from 36% of the market in 1981 to 23% in 1999 continuing a long-running decline from 47% in 1961. The UK and Ireland have also experienced decline or shortage in rental housing. In Ireland, despite a recent (small) growth in housing association stock following the Planning and Development Act 2000, steep rental price increases are evidence of a shortfall in supply and a decline in investment in rental housing especially at the lower end of the market (O'Sullivan, 2001). The UK, and especially England, has experienced a decline in both public and private sector rented housing. Public sector housing declined, by over two million dwellings, from 31% to 21% of the housing stock, following the introduction of 'right-to-buy' policies in 1981. The private rented sector remains very small – 6% in Scotland, 11% in England – and has been declining since the 1950s. There is evidence of an increase in private renting in some metropolitan areas in England during the 1990s arising from the availability of 'housing-to-let' mortgages. However, the sustainability of this component of the rental sector is questionable. There appears to be some correlation between the size of the private rented sector and the incidence of homelessness in the UK. Where there is a large private rented sector the incidence of reported homelessness tends to be lower (Pawson, 2000; Kemp et al, 2001).

In contrast, the level of rental housing has been increasing in the Nordic countries. In Finland the rental sector increased from 21% in 1980 to 30% in 1998. However, there is a suggestion that this is a response to structural problems in the housing market in the early 1990s which led to a large number of mortgage defaulters moving into rental housing, employers (especially in Helsinki) providing accommodation for key workers and individual owners renting out their accommodation (Koev, 2002). The long-run stability of this apparent increase may therefore be questioned. Even with this increase, there remains a shortage of rented accommodation particularly in the Helsinki region such that the queue for rent-controlled ARAVA flats has grown significantly. In Denmark, the rental sector increased from 41% to 44% between 1980 and 2000. This was achieved entirely by an increase in social renting and cooperative housing – private rented accommodation declined from 22% to 18% of the housing stock. Sweden, on the other hand, witnessed a transfer of rental accommodation resulting from the sale of Municipal Housing Companies to private landlords and conversion of rental housing to Tenant Owner Societies. Sweden has had the lowest level of new house construction in Europe throughout the 1990s and the construction of rented accommodation has been most affected. Hence, it is estimated that a third of the population live in municipalities with a shortage of rental housing (National Board of Housing Building and Planning, 2000, p 8).

Elsewhere in Europe the causes underlying the shortage of rental accommodation are more complex involving both market factors and government policy. In Austria rented accommodation built with public subsidy is bound to social allocation criteria for a time-limited period (normally ten years) after which the owner can dispose of the property or rent at unregulated market rents. The majority of private subsidised dwellings now fall outside that restriction period. The systematic decrease in the availability of low-cost apartments was enhanced by the privatisation of formerly publicly supported properties of all kinds including – public housing agencies' apartments, council housing, state-owned industries workers' housing (like VOEST Alpine, Railroad Company) and federal housing for civil servants and military personnel. This development culminated in the recent abolition of the non-profit principle (*Gemeinnuetzigkeit*) of federal housing associations that required them to offer housing for the public good. Legislation in 2001 has changed the non-profit status of housing associations and, as a result, it is estimated that 300,000 social housing units are to be sold to private housing agencies such as private investment funds, banks and insurance companies (Hütter, 2001).

Several decisive changes have also led to the decline in rented accommodation in Germany in recent years. Part of the housing stock owned by municipalities and cooperatives in East Germany in 1993 was sold as a condition laid down by the *Altschuldenhilfegesetz* (a Federal Act which regulates debts of housing societies from the former German Democratic Republic). According to *Kreditanstalt für*

Wiederaufbau (the Credit Institute for Reconstruction), approximately 281,000 dwellings were sold between 1993 and 1999 (Busch-Geertsema, 2001). In West Germany, with the expiry of time-limited social obligations, only 2.3 million social rented housing units remained in 1999 and perhaps only one million social rental dwellings will be left in Germany in 2005 (GDW, 1998, p 23). The remaining social housing stock is, to a great extent, concentrated in specific areas (often in multi-storey blocks on the outskirts of metropolitan cities). At the same time many municipalities being owners or shareholders of social housing companies have completely or partially sold their shares and as a consequence lost influence over the allocation of the dwellings concerned.

Although its market share is declining, the private rented sector in Belgium is still the second most important housing segment in that country. More than one quarter of all households lives in private rental accommodation, while only 6% live in the social rental sector. The consequence is severe waiting lists for social housing. On the other hand, recurrent changes in legislation affecting the power relationship between the tenant and landlord imply that the private rental sector does not offer a stable and appealing housing alternative. De Decker argues that "private letting is only a temporary solution for a majority of households or a solution for individuals and families who have no alternative, for families who are *forced* into private renting" (2001, p 19). Despite the existence of these very real problems, policies have not been introduced to increase the provision of social housing which remains among the lowest in Europe.

It is clear from this account that, while the rented sector is undergoing systemic decline in most countries, the reasons for this decline are varied. It follows from this that the impact of this decline on vulnerable households may also be different and will differ according to the structure of the rental market. The segmentation of the housing market between private and public rental housing is therefore significant to our understanding of the factors affecting the access to affordable housing for vulnerable households.

Segmentation

The segmentation of the rented housing sector has important implications for access to affordable housing for vulnerable groups. However, this segmentation is more complex than the simple distinction between public and private forms of rental tenure, involving as it does factors of ownership, price, security of tenure, allocation and location. In many countries this segmentation is reinforced by differential systems of rent regulation and subsidy.

Kemeny (1995) conceptualises the rental housing systems in Europe as two polar types of strategy towards cost renting. The first strategy, which he terms the 'integrated or unitary rental market', is a classic example of the social market philosophy. The aim is to keep the profit motive but to ameliorate it as much as possible by encouraging non-profit forms of rental housing. The result, according to Kemeny, is a mixed market in which social and economic considerations both play a part in determining the supply and demand of housing. The second, polar opposite strategy, he describes as the 'dualist rental system'. The distinguishing characteristic of this system is the parallel existence of public and private rental systems subject to increasingly divergent forms of provision and conditions of tenure. This strategy comprises two separate systems – one more or less regulated private rental market and a public means-tested allocation system. According to Kemeny "it is precisely those countries that have a residual welfare provision that also tend to have a dualist rental system" (1995, p 63). He includes in this category – the UK (especially England), Ireland, the Mediterranean countries and Finland. He identifies five countries as possessing unitary rental markets – Austria, Denmark, Germany, the Netherlands and Sweden. Kemeny's categorisation makes no mention of France, Belgium or Luxembourg.

The dualist rental strategy has important implications for how government manages the owner-occupied sector and on the nature of the private rented sector. Kemeny describes a 'ratchet effect' (1995, pp 54-5) which extends home ownership to ever more marginal households as a result of the combined effect of a shortage of cost rent housing and/or differential subsidies. The ratchet effect, which leads to the emergence of low-income owner-occupation, encourages the expansion of a form of petty landlordism. Private renting thus includes a proportion of landlords who are owners renting their main home for short periods, or rooms within them, to eke out mortgage payments or compensate for low pensions. These owners are concerned to select tenants carefully and to deny them security of tenure. Kemeny further suggests that this effect is more noticeable when the home ownership rate exceeds two thirds of households.

The impact of market segmentation on vulnerable households is apparent in a number of countries within the dualist or residual welfare regime. Tosi (2001) describes a highly segmented rental market in Italy. The rental sector includes public sector owned social housing, public sector property in the for-profit sector and privately owned property. This results in different forms of rental contract: social rents, rents negotiated by tenants' associations, 'unofficial' contracts and free market contracts (CNEL, 1997). This system of protected rent contracts and free market rents creates rigidity in the market resulting in fewer dwellings coming onto the market and lower levels of residential mobility. Moving house can result in a considerable increase in the cost of housing (Coppo, 1998). Hence the opportunity for marginal households to gain access to (the small proportion of) low-rent protected tenancies is restricted. This rigidity and segmentation is witnessed in the increase in end-of-contract eviction orders sought in the courts which have been so high as to periodically lead the government to freeze evictions. Ireland's rental market is divided into a high-rent unregulated profit market offering no security of tenure and a command economy or public rental system with heavily restricted 'poor law' access (O'Sullivan, 2001). The effect of the rigidity of this segmentation is evident in the recent period of economic growth. Increased house prices led to a higher demand for private renting, and hence higher rents. Higher rents in the private rented sector, and the decreasing affordability of new houses, allied to sluggish local authority output has led to 5,000 new additions onto the local authority housing waiting lists each year. In Greece, where over 80% of housing is owner-occupied and government policy promotes home ownership for all, the (small) rental sector is heavily dependent on middle to low-income owners, denying tenants security of tenure.

The unitary rental market, on the other hand, allows a mix of cost-renting and profit-renting to emerge with a maturation of rents at a competitive cost to provide a realistic renting alternative to owner-occupation for a significant proportion of households (Kemeny, 1995). However, the shift of dwellings from subsidised cost renting to the profit rental sector, which appears from the evidence above to be occurring in Austria and Germany, is likely to create market rents that are not affordable to marginal households. Therefore, in these situations, government is led to develop a new restricted access, means-tested rental sector – creating in effect a dualist system. Whether this occurs will depend on whether the transformation of public subsidised rental housing to the private sector (that is, the harmonisation of cost rent and market rent) occurs at a point where the maturation of the debt allows cost rent housing to remain competitive with market rents. There is thus evidence that, in unitary rental markets, governments are creating a more targeted and means tested rental system. In Germany, as publicly subsidised housing reverts to the private sector, new legislation in 2002 identifies low-income groups, homeless persons and other persons in need of support as target groups for the support of rented housing (Busch-Geertsema, 2001). In Austria, Schoibl (2001) refers to segmentation in relation to differences in security of tenure. In Denmark it has been stated that the aim of housing policy is to ensure the provision of adequate housing for those on low incomes and other disadvantaged groups in society (Danish Ministry of Housing and Building, 1984). In the Netherlands the social housing sector was never targeted solely at lower income households. Over time, the proportion of households on higher incomes in the social sector has grown considerably. This has now become a major issue as household formation rates have continued to grow more rapidly than in other countries.

Housing costs and housing allowances

It has been argued that housing costs are becoming more expensive relative to incomes over the medium term, even when cyclical effects are discounted (Ball, 1999). The reasons for this phenomenon are complex but are normally associated with the decrease in generic subsidies, relaxation in rent controls and increased reliance on private sector borrowing by social housing agencies (Haffner and Van der Heijden, 2000). Given the differences between countries in ways of defining housing expenditure, in identifying subsidies and measuring the value of housing assistance, comparisons of the levels of housing expenditure and the composition of this expenditure between countries is difficult. However, a number of authors identify common trends over time in different countries and in particular the shift from supply-side to demand-side subsidies is apparent (Oxley and Smith, 1996; Van der Heijden, 2002). Many countries attempt to offset the decline in supply (property based) subsidies by extending targeted consumption subsidies (housing allowances). This should lead to greater protection of low-income and vulnerable groups by compensating for the increasing level of housing expenditure on a means-tested basis.

Housing allowance systems vary between countries both in terms of their objectives and purposes and in terms of the policy instruments and institutional arrangements employed. Equally there is variation in the relationship between income-related support for housing costs and other forms of social assistance. Comparison of housing allowance systems is available elsewhere (Kemp, 1990; Oxley and Smith, 1996). The important aspects to highlight in relation to our concern here with access to affordable housing are:

- the increasing dependence on housing allowances as a result of the subsidy shifts (discussed earlier in this chapter);
- the regressive impact of housing allowances.

Furthermore, where benefit replacement rates are high (rent allowance falls as employment income increases) those in low-wage employment may be most affected (MacLennan et al, 1996). It has also been argued that this shift from object subsidies to subject subsidies has helped to polarise housing (Priemus and Dieleman, 1999; Gibb, 2002).

The shift to subject subsidies has resulted in a growing dependency on housing allowances and a growth in this form of housing expenditure. Housing allowances as a proportion of housing expenditure grew in France from 24% in 1980 to 50% in 1997, in Germany from 11% in 1980 to 30% in 1992 and by a similar proportion in the UK. In the Netherlands the number of recipients of rent subsidy increased by 26% between 1985 and 1997 while expenditure in housing allowances increased by over 80% (De Feijter, 2001). In Finland housing allowances are directed through three distinct schemes at pensioners, students and rental households. The three forms of housing allowance taken together doubled between 1990 and 1995, at a time when housing expenditure grew by almost 50%. Since that time allowances have remained static while total housing subsidies have declined to 1990 levels. Hence, allowances now constitute almost one half of total subsidies compared to about one quarter in 1990 (Kärkkäinen, 2001). Similar growth patterns can also be identified in Austria and Belgium.

This pattern, however, has not been universal in Europe with Sweden and Denmark appearing to diverge from this trend. One of the cornerstones of traditional Swedish housing policy was a generous tenure-neutral system of housing allowances. However, concordant with the general reduction in housing subsidies, housing allowances in Sweden have decreased both in terms of the number of recipients and the total value. Between 1995 and 1999, the number of couples with children in receipt of allowances declined by two thirds and by over a half for single adults under 29 years of age. By 1999 more than a half of recipients of housing allowances were single parents. Housing allowances have increased only marginally (by around 8%) in Denmark during the 1990s. Rent allowances (one third of recipients) are targeted at older households, while rent subsidies (two thirds of recipients) are mainly targeted at households with children in the rental sector (80% of all rent subsidy recipients). The number of households receiving housing benefits has remained stable since 1994.

Within the context of these changes in the importance of housing allowances, three main trends are evident in relation to the impact of housing costs on vulnerable households. First, the (net) rent burden has increased overall; second, those on the lowest incomes pay proportionately more of their income on direct housing costs; third, there is an increasing proportion of households for whom (net) housing costs are unaffordable. Furthermore, there is some evidence to suggest that this inequality appears to be getting worse over time.

The proportion that net rent comprises of net household income has been growing over time in northern Europe and (though to a lesser degree) in southern Europe. The situation in northern Europe is described well by Van der Heijden and Haffner (2000) who, in a study of six EU countries – Belgium, West Germany, France, the Netherlands, Sweden and the UK – consider the changes in income, gross rent and net rent (net of housing allowances). They demonstrate that, during the early 1990s, the increase in net rents was larger than the growth in disposable incomes in both the social and private housing sectors. In countries with very low levels of rented accommodation (southern Europe mainly) it is typically the case that a small protected or regulated rented sector, available to only a very small sector of the population, has been cushioned from large rent increases. However, for most households in those countries, reliant on home ownership or private rented housing, net housing expenditure has increased. In Ireland, rents rose by 300% between 1990 and 2000 while average incomes rose by 8% per annum. Data from the Household Budget Survey in Portugal shows a growth in average family expenditure on housing from 5.4% in 1980 to 21% in the late 1990s. Sharp increases in house prices and a marked reduction in protected housing in Spain has had a deleterious effect on the ratio of housing costs to income since the early 1990s (Carbrera, 2001). Similar changes are reported in Italy (Tosi, 2001).

While the net rent burden has been increasing, it is evident that those in the lower income bands are paying the largest proportion of net income on direct housing costs. For example, Van der Heijden and Haffner (2000) conclude that the average net rent increase was greater in the lower income deciles compared to higher income groups in both public and private sectors and in all six countries they studied. The example of Italy can be cited to demonstrate that the situation in southern Europe is broadly similar. Tosi (2001) quotes a recent survey by Sunia (1999) to argue that rent is negatively correlated with income. Overall the percentage of income paid on rent (12%) is low compared to elsewhere in Europe. However, analysis by income band shows that, in 1998, the rent–income ratio was over 30% for more than half the households in the lowest income group while it was less than half that proportion for the majority of households in the highest income bands.

This increase in the rent burden over time implies that housing is becoming less affordable for an increasing proportion of households if we assume that 25% of income is an affordable level of expenditure on direct net housing costs. Busch-Geertsema (2001) calculates that, between 1993 and 1998, the proportion of households spending more than 35% of their net income on rent rose from 18% to 27% in West Germany and from 5% to 17% in East Germany. De Feijter (2001) quotes evidence that 39% of those in the lowest income quartile in the Netherlands paid more than 25% of their income on net rent in 1990 compared to 59% in 1998. In the UK, the

> ... existence of a housing benefit system which can pay all of the rent in the social rented sector clearly affects the affordability issue for those on the lowest incomes but creates its own problems relating to benefit dependency and the poverty trap. (Aldridge, 2001, p 13)

One of the results of the increased rent burden is a growing number of households in rent arrears and a substantial increase in the number of legal cases for eviction. As a result, Busch-Geertsema argues that, in North Rhine-Westphalia, "while the number of homeless people has been reduced the number of households in serious risk of homelessness has increased substantially" (2001, p 18). Increases in evictions are also an issue of increasing debate in Sweden and the UK in recent years.

Within countries the impact of differential regional economic growth affects this picture adversely for vulnerable households in high growth areas (see Chapter Three of this volume). Regional cost differentials are described in Austria as resulting both from economic factors and from policy differences between the federal provinces (Schoibl, 2001). Furthermore, housing costs, including rents, tend to be higher in the major cities and this occurs both in countries with regulated or controlled rents (for example, Helsinki in Finland) and in countries with less marked rent regulation (for example, the cities of Milan, Rome and Naples in Italy).

The impact of changing demographic and household structures is evident in that some types of household are more vulnerable to rising housing costs and find it more difficult to afford decent and adequate housing. Dual income households should be more able to cope with the shocks of rising housing costs but, in northern European countries especially, the largest growth in household formation is among single person (that is, single income) households. In both Finland (Kärkkäinen, 2001) and Sweden (Sahlin, 2001) it is suggested that single adults tend to pay a greater proportion of their income on housing and that, during the 1990s, the relative cost of housing has increased more for these households than for other groups. While single parents and single older people benefit from social protection, single adults of working age are more exposed. Kärkkäinen (2001) suggests that, in Finland, changes during the 1990s in housing allowance systems negatively affected one-person households in particular. Sahlin (quoting Turner, 2000) argues that the increasing proportion of disposable income spent on housing during the 1990s is the result of the dismantling of housing policy which "affected low income households more than the average families and singles more than couples" (Turner, 2000, p 18).

Access to social housing

The increasing uncertainty and volatility in the housing market and the declining importance of the private rented sector in most countries emphasises the pivotal role of social housing provision in meeting the needs of low-income and vulnerable households and in facilitating access to decent and affordable housing. Although the social housing sector, where it exists, is essential to facilitate low-income accessibility, quality and affordability it is equally evident that there are clear exclusionary processes at work. After four decades as the engine of low-income housing policies, the social sector is in decline across most of western Europe and is increasingly associated with the 'new poor' and has become a critical locus of 'social exclusion' (MacLennan et al, 1996). At the same time, government investment in social housing has been allowed to leak out into the private sector through sale to sitting tenants and transfer of property to co-ownership agencies.

It is suggested that social housing has increasingly come to be targeted at specific vulnerable groups (the homeless, the elderly, single parents, immigrants, low-income households), with the implication that it is taking on a more welfare or residual role (MacLennan et al, 1996; Priemus and Boelhouwer, 1999). However, models of provision, ownership, financing and management are changing and increasingly adopting market principles. Equally, allocation mechanisms are increasingly responding to factors other than direct housing need. Market factors associated with the increased use of private finance, on the one hand, and political factors associated with policies of social inclusion, on the other hand, lead to policies of social balance in allocation and tenure mix in new development. This section examines the implications of these trends for access to affordable housing for vulnerable and homeless households.

Allocation of housing

The increasing use of private finance and the need for providers to use their own reserves to fund development and renovation affects the accessibility of vulnerable households to affordable housing by direct and indirect effects on allocation policies. Business methods associated with financial and treasury management have been increasingly adopted by housing associations, which results in risk-averse decisions regarding the location and type of development undertaken as well as in allocation and housing management decisions. The increased reliance on reserves and asset management has led to a growth in the size of housing associations to achieve the economies of scale required in a competitive market. Mixed funding and risk sharing leads to increased regulation and performance standards regarding rent arrears, vacancy and turnover levels which also leads to more risk-averse decisions regarding housing allocation. While these factors hinder access to the social housing sector for the lowest income groups, this form of prevention of access relies also on other motivations, of which the goal of a balanced social mix is most frequently cited[1].

Municipal ownership of social housing allows direct implementation of social housing objectives by central and local government. Where social housing is owned by municipal companies or by housing associations, or is provided by social sector subsidies to private agencies, municipal control requires a regulatory system and statutory or local cooperation agreements. Regulatory controls are implemented through the use of performance standards which must balance issues of building quality, financial requirements (for example, resulting from the increased use of private finance) and rent control as well as meeting the housing needs of specific groups. There is evidence from all countries that tighter control on levels of rent arrears coupled with rising (real) rents has led to increasing eviction and tighter controls on tenant probity during the allocation process. Typically, housing associations will be required to meet arrears targets of around 2% of the rent roll. Housing management targets (reducing vacancies in the housing stock and reducing housing turnover) can also work to the disadvantage of some groups and particularly young single adults who may have difficulty sustaining a tenancy.

The influence of government on housing allocation works at different levels. First, legislation in some countries has, recently, defined specific target groups for social housing. In Denmark, since 1994 social housing is targeted at low-income groups and pensioners. In Germany, legislation introduced in 2002 identifies defined groups of households as the target for the shrinking social housing sector. These include households already provided for in legislation – pregnant women, large families, young couples, single parents, the elderly, severely disabled – and now makes explicit reference to "the homeless and other persons in need of support" (BMVBW, 2001, p 34). In Scotland, the Housing Act (2001) places a statutory duty on housing associations to assist local authorities in housing homeless people and restricts to very limited circumstances the reasons for which a housing association can legitimately refuse a homeless referral or nomination. In England housing associations have successfully resisted the inclusion of such an obligation in the Homelessness Act (2002). However, the legislation in England widens the statutory definition of priority need for social housing to include homeless teenagers aged 16-17, care leavers aged 18-21, people vulnerable as a result of an institutionalised care background, and people fleeing violence or threat of violence and ex-offenders. In Italy, since 1992 (Law 179/1992), a percentage of social housing (both *edilizia sovvenzionata* and *edilizia agevolata*) are reserved for particular categories of persons. The categories cited in the act include the elderly, large families, immigrants, students and, in some regions, young couples and new families. However, the regions are responsible for defining which categories are prioritised and it is unlikely that all these categories (for example, immigrants) will be prioritised at the regional level.

Second, eligibility for government subsidy is normally tied to a condition of municipal nomination rights to a proportion of the housing stock. The structure of a national or regional regulatory agency, municipal authorities and a multiplicity of social landlords, while it may create choice, leads to diversity of practice. In the UK some local authorities and housing associations have experimented (with mixed success) with 'common housing registers'. However, even here the landlords retain different allocation policies and priorities. The ability of the regulatory agency or local authorities to monitor housing need and allocation practices is therefore limited. Nomination agreements are most needed and yet are least effective in situations where housing demand is greatest and where there is a shortage of social housing. Evidence from the UK (Pawson and Third, 1997; Edgar, 2002) shows a clear regional variation in the effectiveness of nomination agreements in providing for statutory homeless households that reflect geographical patterns of housing market demand. A recent study in Finland shows that municipal council housing has a higher level of unemployed and low-income tenants compared to housing associations despite nomination rights and income ceiling criteria (Laukkanen, 1998). For this reason, the most recent Homelessness Policy established, by decree, a 20% allocation right for municipalities (10% in Helsinki).

Third, local cooperation agreements between municipalities and social housing landlords provide a further mechanism for government to influence housing allocation in favour of vulnerable groups. In Germany, although landlords generally have a free choice among applicants who hold a certificate of entitlement from the local housing office (*Wohnberechtigungsschein*) this is restricted in areas of housing need providing the municipality with greater nomination rights. However, there is no national overview on the distribution and use of allocation rights. A recent study (BBR, 2000) shows that three fifths of municipalities have some form of cooperation agreement with housing associations to provide households in urgent need with accommodation. Only half of these agreements are contractual and about one third have fixed quota arrangements to let a proportion of vacant dwellings to specific groups including the homeless.

A number of countries have established income ceilings to prescribe eligibility to social housing (for example in Finland, Germany, the Netherlands, France and Italy). The problem here is to prescribe income ceilings that are neither too broad nor too narrow and to ensure these are regularly up-rated with real wage inflation. In Germany income ceilings allow access to social housing for 40% of the population. Once a household has moved into a social house it is allowed to stay even when its income has risen. Despite the use of a fee to be paid by tenants when their incomes rise above a certain level (*Fehlbelegungsabgabe*) tenants have not moved out of social housing. This suggests an increasing distributional problem where relatively high-income earners occupy low-cost social housing while low-income households must seek solutions in the relatively more expensive private sector (Oxley and Smith, 1996).

One result of the decline in social housing has been the fear of concentration of deprived groups in some (low demand, poorer quality) housing estates with consequent segregation and stigmatisation effects. Therefore, at the same time as legislation is targeting social housing on those in greatest need, fears of segregation, 'overstrained neighbourhoods' and the traditional goal of a 'balanced social mix' in the occupancy of social housing have gained influence in the public discourse about housing policies. The concept of social balance or mix is to be found in legislation and in guidance in many countries but the definition of the term is seldom discussed in detail. The impact of such an approach will differ depending on the spatial scale at which it is applied. In France, the imbalance in the geographical distribution of social housing led to proactive responses to provide a minimum specific quota in communes of a certain size (the 1991 Town Planning Outline Act) and to highlight the need for concerted action on the allocation of social housing (the 1998 Outline Act on the Prevention of the Various Forms of Exclusion). More recently, the Urban Solidarity and Renewal Act (December 2000) strengthens the earlier legislation and requires communes to provide a minimum 20% quota of social housing by a certain deadline or face penalties. Sociologists in Germany argue that a share of 15% of 'minority households' in a given area acts as a 'critical threshold' for a dramatic increase in conflicts in the neighbourhood (Eichner, 1998, p 42). This has been used in typical guidelines, in the past, at the tenement level to suggest "not more than two foreigner households per entrance" (Hubert and Tomann, 1991, p 27). In the UK, studies have similarly argued for critical thresholds for child density in multi-storey flats. In Denmark the National Organisation for Social Housing, aiming at a more balanced mix, has attempted to make social housing more attractive to higher income groups by, for example, allowing 20% equity holding and allowing innovations in design. This has had a direct effect on waiting lists for more needy households. Local lettings schemes have been piloted in England to provide a basis for housing allocation that takes account of factors other than individual housing need in the allocation process. So far these are small scale and encompass only a small number of local authorities often including council estates in areas of low demand. In Finland, housing allocation procedures (especially in the Helsinki region) have attempted to prevent concentration of deprived households by a variety of methods. The present composition of occupants in a block of flats is taken into account when new occupants are chosen (this also occurs in France). Equally the sale of municipal housing to cooperatives in Denmark has revealed long-term consequences. Surveys of cooperative members have revealed negative attitudes towards vulnerable groups as future tenants and thus the exercise of social control (aimed at retaining a social balance and social stability) removes these dwellings from access by vulnerable groups. There is evidence that the composition of cooperative tenants is changing with reductions in the proportion of pensioner and unemployed households.

In her detailed study on landlords' exclusionary practices in Sweden, Sahlin (2001) points out that the rental housing market should not be confused with a market for consumer goods or capital. In the latter case, customers do not have to justify their choice of goods and producers, and the providers have no reason to prefer one customer to another except for the prices they are willing to pay. The rental housing market differs (the public sector as well as the private sector), since the product is the "right to dwell in a specific flat or house for an undetermined period of time" (p 49), and for which the price is paid repeatedly and continuously. Therefore, Sahlin argues that "for the producer/landlord, it is crucial that new tenants are reliable rent-payers and do not cause trouble or costs through material damage, neighbour conflicts or a status loss for the house/area" (2001, p 57). These requirements give rise to a set of implicitly and explicitly used criteria for rejection of tenants who are considered to be non-profitable in the short or long term. In particular, Sahlin stresses that the Swedish municipal housing companies have long since – and partly thanks to their cooperative relationship with local authorities – kept their own extensive records on tenant's behaviour, which they can communicate to interested new landlords. In her research, Sahlin found covert as well as overt criteria for rejection among the municipal housing companies. Making a distinction between formal and informal methods, she outlines the nature of overt and covert screening methods (see Figure 4.1). Sahlin's distinction between formal and informal methods rely on the difference between a clear and formal communication about the negative result of the candidate's application, while informal methods are to be associated with the lack of a clear judgement towards the applicant, even when they are based on overt criteria.

Gatekeepers are also at work on the German social housing market. Busch-Geertsema refers to the widespread discrimination by excluding strategies of public landlords. All in all, he states, it may be summarised that there are large groups of households facing discrimination in the housing market because of their demographic and social characteristics and their nationality. There are also smaller groups of households which face much stricter exclusion because they are seen as "problem groups" and "trouble makers" or as persons "unable to live independently" (Busch-Geertsema, 2001, p 23-7). In France, HLM organisations are required by law to ensure tenants have the financial capacity to pay their rent. This profit-led logic (or at least a logic that does not tolerate deficits) prevents or limits the access to the social housing segment for the weakest income groups, despite the *loi Besson* (1990) or the law on fighting social exclusion (1998) (Betton, 2001, p 26-7). In the UK, following the 1996 Housing Act, there has been an increase in the use of 'non-secure' tenancies by local authorities. In England, following the 1996 Housing Act, local authority lettings in secure tenancies decreased by half (from 240,000 per year to 120,000 by 2001). At the same time, lettings in non-secure tenancies quadrupled (from 20,000 per year to over 100,000 in 2001) of which 80% were 'introductory' or 'starter' tenancies aimed at ensuring that only 'reliable' tenants are offered secure, permanent tenancies.

Figure 4.1: Allocation criteria in social housing

		METHODS OF REJECTION	
		Formal	**Informal**
CRITERIA	**Overt**	*Screening for info on over criteria (debts, income, evictions, and so on)*	*Discouragement from applying*
	Covert	*Individual judgements ("You don't fit in") ("We'll call you back")*	*Holding back info on vacancies, non-decisions*

Source: Sahlin (2001, p 58)

Access to affordable social housing is thus constrained by the reduction in provision and by the impact of tighter control on risk management exercised by social landlords and their regulatory agencies. The objectives of social inclusion, social balance and accountability which social housing is tasked to achieve are, as this description suggests, often in conflict. An important component in reconciling these objectives is the provision of support to vulnerable households to enable them to sustain a tenancy and to overcome some of the obstacles to access.

Housing and support

We argued in a previous volume in this series (Edgar et al, 2000) that housing and financial support are, in themselves, insufficient to meet the needs of individual homeless households. This section considers the nature of support and housing in facilitating access to housing for vulnerable households and the homeless. The need for support linked to housing provision arises from a variety of factors. The shift from the institutional provision of care services (for example, for those with mental health problems or learning disabilities) to delivery of care services in the community, since the 1970s, has been a major structural factor in the growth of this form of housing need. In a parallel, perhaps related, development the provision of homelessness services has shifted from a police or medical model providing emergency services and temporary accommodation, towards a social model aimed at prevention and resettlement and individualised service provision. Even a superficial examination of the complexity of individual pathways into homelessness is sufficient to demonstrate that not all homeless people will require support to re-establish their lives successfully in permanent housing. Equally, however, there are people who are at risk of institutional living or 'rooflessness' in the absence of appropriate transitional or long-term support (see Edgar et al, 2000, pp 138-44). The importance of relationship factors and personal reasons cited by empirical research as causes of homelessness has led some authors to argue that the changing role of the family increasingly requires formal provision of social protection and support by the state. The evidence for this 'commodification of care' is not, yet, evident in all the welfare regimes of Europe and structures of care provision for some support needs are stronger in some countries than in others. However, the process of 'de-familialisation' can be more universally recognised (Esping-Andersen, 1999). It is likely therefore that access to housing for some vulnerable individuals and households will increasingly require the formal (state provided or state funded) provision of supported housing or of support linked to appropriate housing.

While there has been a significant growth in support in housing in many countries in Europe it remains the case that there is an under-provision related to need and that the existing provision tends to be geographically disparate demonstrating, in particular, a clear urban bias. Hence the actual availability of provision will, of itself, limit access.

We have argued elsewhere that there are three broad groupings of countries in which supported housing has a distinctive genesis, relationship to social welfare services and housing policy (Edgar et al, 2000, pp 190-2). In one group of countries (the Nordic countries, the Netherlands, Germany and the UK) the emergence of support in housing has been associated with the de-institutionalisation of care services. In these countries the form of provision is more likely to be designated to particular purposes through a combination of physical form, management and funding mechanisms. Indeed in some instances it is linked to a 'staircase of transition' model leading from institutional forms of support to community-oriented support provision. Allocation procedures in these situations tend to be restrictive and to be prescribed in the policy and funding instruments that have been used to develop the service. There is evidence, in almost all these countries, of recent legislation that aims to 'support people' and to uncouple the funding of support from particular forms of accommodation. This should lead to a system of allocation determined by housing need rather than by the institutional history of individual applicants. The danger, of course, is that funding will not match the required needs in the community and that even where needs assessments are undertaken these will not adequately 'size the pot' to establish adequate budgets.

The second group of countries shares some of these characteristics in the development of support in housing. However, they are distinguished by the fact that the mechanisms of funding and provision arise more from a social exclusion model. We suggest that France, Belgium and Luxembourg fit this category and that Italy and Austria also fit more easily into this group than any other. Provision in these situations comes through housing and social services structures utilising social inclusion objectives and funding sources. A key feature of provision is the localised origins of development often arising from local coordination between agencies in a bottom-up response to locally perceived needs. This suggests that there is less prescription in relation to target groups and methods of provision and that this is less prescribed in legislation and related implementation instruments. However, the nature of this diversity of provision will also have an impact on access to support and housing for vulnerable groups.

The third group of countries (Greece, Portugal, Spain and Ireland) are characterised by limited de-institutionalisation and a reliance on family and civil society provision of support. Supported housing provision is only weakly developed in these countries. Furthermore, it tends to have developed as transitional accommodation provision from traditional homelessness hostels. The provision is a mixture of new services and coordination arrangements between existing services. The support is clearly defined as transitional often for quite short time periods (typically four months) and often associated with a requirement to accept and retain employment. Access to support is thus clearly prescribed and focussed on specific homeless (often male-oriented) needs.

A key distinction in the provision of support services is that between 'ambulatory' and 'stationary' support or, to put it another way, between supported accommodation and support in housing. In countries with a longer history of supported housing provision there is a marked shift away from designated physical forms of 'special needs' housing towards 'floating' support services that follow the person rather than being attached to particular housing or forms of accommodation. The effectiveness of this model is predicated on two key policy developments. First, it requires a shift in funding responsibilities (from health or social protection to local social services). Second, it relies on the effective coordination between (municipal) social services and local housing agencies (public, voluntary and private). With regard to the latter, access to housing for those who are deemed to need support to sustain a tenancy is therefore dependent on prior access to appropriate support services. Housing allocation mechanisms may therefore be determined by criteria other than direct or objective assessment of housing need. The development of joint assessment mechanisms and the use of personal care plans that include housing and support needs are still in their infancy in most countries in Europe. Access to housing, in these circumstances, is therefore constrained by social services' funding availability even in a situation of housing surplus. Furthermore, there is evidence that, irrespective of actual budget constraints, the mechanisms by which social services authorities commission services can lead to under-occupancy of available accommodation (Audit Commission, 1998; Edgar and Mina-Coull, 1998) and therefore limit access to housing for some vulnerable households. In all countries the problem of dealing with individuals with challenging behaviour (for example, some people with mental health problems, learning disability or alcohol/drug dependency) or of antisocial or problem families is proving an intractable problem. Good practice evidence in family mediation and in support systems and housing forms that can ameliorate these challenges remain exceptional.

Access to support is intended to be a positive response to the housing needs of marginalised and vulnerable households that aims either to facilitate resettlement or, in the best situation, to prevent homelessness. However, the assessment procedures involved and the increased regulation and management of individual lifestyles can also hold dangers. In Sweden, for example, where supported housing is often offered in tenancy arrangements that form 'special contracts' some authors have suggested there is a danger of creating a 'secondary housing market' – a market of exclusion (Sahlin, 1999). In England, there has been an increasing use of non-secure local authority tenancies since 1996, 80% of which take the form of 'starter tenancies' offered for a defined 'probationary' period. There is clearly a danger that, in the absence of support or where support fails, vulnerable households may be excluded from mainstream housing with normal tenancies and security of tenure.

Conclusion

Insecurity and vulnerability in the housing market arises not just from the changes in the market but also from the changing role of the state. The withdrawal of the state from direct intervention to indirect animation, doing less and enabling more, has created a more complex picture of housing vulnerability than simply a division between the majority who are well housed and the circumstances of the most disadvantaged who are badly housed or homeless. The changing role of the state in the housing market may be crudely characterised as a shift from the policies of redistribution in the heyday of the welfare state to the procedures of risk management in the era of regulated delegation in the 1990s. Increasing uncertainty and volatility in the private housing market combined with increased risk management and business-led decisions in the public sector creates a division between the securely housed, the insecurely housed and the excluded.

The provision of affordable social housing is the most direct and effective means of guaranteeing access to housing for those in the worst housing conditions and for the homeless. In countries with minimal social housing provision (the Mediterranean countries, Belgium, Luxembourg and Ireland) policies to improve access to decent and affordable housing by this approach are exceptional. In Portugal, social housing has been provided to remove shanty housing that has concentrated in Lisbon and Porto; it has nevertheless resulted in a significant increase in social housing provision in that country. In Ireland, social housing programmes have been revived to increase the supply of affordable rented housing, especially in the Dublin region. In Finland the programme to reduce homelessness is perceived to rely on adequate levels of social housing provision. Elsewhere social housing has either been reduced through policies of sales (the UK), the ending of time-limited subsidies (Germany, Austria) or through transfer of ownership (the UK, Sweden). At the same time the changing institutional structure of social landlords, especially where housing associations are the key agents, has resulted in greater emphasis on risk management in all aspects of housing development, housing management and financial control. The effects of both the reduction in social housing provision and the tighter gate-keeping controls exercised in its allocation and management work to the detriment of the most vulnerable.

The decline in the rental housing sector in most countries, even in countries with relatively low levels of rental housing stock, is a factor in creating housing vulnerability for low-income and marginal groups. The segmentation of the rented sector is crucial in determining the availability of affordable housing for the most vulnerable. The decline in rented housing emphasises the pivotal role of social housing and yet allocation mechanisms are increasingly responding to factors other than direct housing need. The nature of the governance of social housing has, in many cases, created financial pressures and performance standards which emphasise practices of risk management leading to overt and covert screening methods in housing allocation. The private rented sector has an important role to play in meeting the housing needs of particular types of household at different stages in their life course. The young, new households, single adults and households reconstructing after separation or divorce are often more dependent on this sector. Equally, households who are not eligible for social housing will have to rely on the private sector if home ownership is not a feasible option. This will include, for example, those in work on low incomes who fall just outside income thresholds for social housing and those who have been evicted from social housing, those who do not have residence or citizenship qualification. However, there is evidence from a range of countries from northern and southern Europe that the most vulnerable need support in gaining and sustaining a tenancy in the private rental sector.

The increase in housing costs in recent years has created a situation in which housing represents a high and increasing proportion of household income. Those in low-paid employment as well as those lacking stable employment are most vulnerable to housing indebtedness and typically pay a higher proportion of their net household income on direct housing costs than do more affluent households. Faced with a lack of affordable housing, households in insecure employment or on low incomes have limited options. They can either reduce their consumption of housing – occupying lower quality and cheaper housing – or they can reduce their consumption of other goods and services. Housing allowances, where they exist, protect defined categories of household. Nevertheless, there is a clear trend in many countries of increasing levels of evictions due to rent arrears and of mortgage repossessions. Indebtedness arising from housing costs or difficulty in affording decent housing may affect people because of their household status, their position in the labour market or their situation related to social protection systems in their country. Therefore, for example, households relying on a single income can be expected to pay a higher proportion of that income on housing – single adult households are an increasing proportion of the household structure in many countries and especially in major conurbations. Households relying on low-paid, seasonal or unstable employment where social protection systems do not protect a minimum income will also be at risk. So too will households entering or leaving the labour market (the young and the retired) where social protection systems do not provide support for housing costs.

The availability of housing and the financial support to pay for it are not in themselves sufficient to guarantee access to housing for the homeless and the most vulnerable in our society. The growth of supported housing (and support in housing) has been important in both preventing homelessness and in the resettlement of homeless people and in enabling people to sustain a tenancy. In most countries the availability of support or of supported accommodation is still substantially less than actual need. Equally, available supply is concentrated in major conurbations and urban areas. Therefore access to housing with support is, for the majority of households who require it, an unrealisable expectation at the moment. Even where support is available, there is a danger that methods of funding and the creation of special housing contracts rather than normal tenancies can create a secondary housing market for vulnerable, homeless households especially those with challenging behaviour or unusual lifestyles.

Note

[1] For a critique and discussion of this concept see Sarkassian (1976) and Jupp (1999).

FIVE

Coping with vulnerability

Creating vulnerability

The European housing market has undergone significant change over the past two decades. This has led to a reconfiguration of housing tenures in all countries. Driven by a process of (re)commodification, Europe has witnessed a universal growth in home ownership, a reshaping of, and a reduction in, the provision of social housing together with complex changes in the privately rented sector where decline and over-supply in some regions contrasts with modest increases and shortages in other (predominantly metropolitan) areas. These changes, as demonstrated in Chapters Three and Four of this volume, have set the conditions for housing vulnerability for significant sections of the population in that each of these tenure categories has a modus operandi which raises barriers, and limits access for certain categories of people.

Access to owner-occupation, based on 'ability to pay' criteria, has the effect of keeping out poorer, less well-paid sections of society. Access to social housing, based on criteria of need, is generally more accessible to poorer families, but can neglect sections of society such as young single people whose needs, as welfare retrenchment encourages the adoption of benefits targeting, are considered to be less pressing. Social housing allocations can also be discriminatory with restricted access to certain ethnic or 'immigrant' groups or those judged to be undeserving because of the attribution of some social stigma such as 'problem family' due to debt arrears or antisocial behaviour. The location of housing can also operate in an exclusionary manner, most obviously in relation to those communities that monitor incomers and operate a covert and sometimes overt system of vetting potential residents. At the other end of the social scale, location can contribute to exclusion in that a community or neighbourhood is branded as a 'ghetto' or 'sink estate' in which residents are effectively trapped and experience prolonged and often extreme forms of social isolation. Housing vulnerability is a condition of those who are denied access to adequate housing through the established channels of provision (the market and the state). It is an inherent condition of homelessness, and it also characterises those who are driven to the margins of the private market and of social housing and forced to occupy, for want of alternatives, relatively high-cost and inadequate accommodation. It is also a condition of those who fall through the market/state nexus and are obliged to look for accommodation outside the established channels, in 'civil society', among friends and relatives, in informal shelters and in charitable hostels.

The experience of, and susceptibility to, housing vulnerability is most prevalent among the poor, among those with no job, or in low-paid employment with few of the skills demanded in an increasingly flexible labour market. The risk of housing vulnerability has, however, also been heightened by the cumulative and continuing effects of what are now well-established changes in the social and demographic structure of European societies. In particular changes in household structures have led to an undermining of the traditional supportive role of the family, exposing previously protected segments of the population to the risk of homelessness. The risk of housing vulnerability is also heightened at different stages in people's lives, by life course events and transitions – loss of a job, family break up, divorce or separation or retirement. And, because of enduring deficiencies in the social fabric and structures of society, some individuals with inherited or socially assigned characteristics (race, disability, gender, sexual orientation) are more susceptible than others to being denied access to adequate housing.

Socio-demographic change and life course transitions

The well-established, but nevertheless profound, changes in the socio-demographic make-up of European society, reflecting accumulated and continuing transformations wrought by what has been called the second demographic transition (Lesthaeghe, 1995), have exposed some hitherto protected groups to the vagaries of the marketplace. The welfare state (including housing) has been unable to accommodate this new burden placed on it.

Five key and defining characteristics of Europe's contemporary demography can be identified (Samers and Woods, 1998, pp 241-3). First, across Europe there has been a decline in fertility and mortality to near replacement levels. The high degree of inter-regional convergence in this context is illustrated by the dramatic declines in fertility in countries such as Italy, Greece and Spain, which had previously experienced rapid population growth. In these countries the total fertility rate is now 1.4, among the lowest in Europe.

Second, life expectancy, reflecting the impact of welfare state provision of medical care, has improved significantly. Infant mortality has declined to as low as eight per 1,000 live births in Greece and Portugal and to seven in France, Germany and Spain, while in Sweden and Finland it is already below five. West Europeans now have among the highest life expectancy of any of the world's populations, varying from a high of over 80 years for females in Sweden to a low of about 70 for males in Portugal.

Third, the continued decline in fertility and increases in life expectancy have led to the ageing of Europe's population with considerable implications in terms of the impact on labour force structures, rising dependency ratios and increased demands on health and welfare services. Across the EU between 18% and 20% of the population are over 60 years of age, and projections into the second decade of the 21st century indicate that the proportion under 15 years of age will fall to below 18% (compared with 25% in the 1970s).

Fourth, all EU countries have experienced an increase in the number of female workers, a trend encouraged by the decline in traditionally male, industrial jobs and an increase in service occupations. Female labour force participation is linked, however, with significant increases, associated with the movement identified in Chapter Three, towards a more flexible labour force, in part-time and casual employment.

Fifth, new patterns of household formation have emerged most significantly leading to the break-up of the 'traditional' male breadwinner/women carers at home household (Paugam, 1998). The impact of economic restructuring and especially deindustrialisation, has undermined the 'stability' of this traditional household type and in its place a plethora of household types have emerged – single parent households, younger single households, older households – reflecting decreased fertility, increased levels of cohabitation, delayed marriage, and increases in the divorce rate. These households are potentially vulnerable to housing risk in that they are frequently associated with the absence of a secure income either in the form of earned pay or benefit payments. The demise of the male breadwinner household has also, importantly, exposed some women to the vagaries of the labour market constraining their ability to form and sustain independent households (see Edgar et al, 2001). Other changes such as those associated with immigration and asylum seeking have had their impact as well – vulnerability among these groups is associated with low or no pay and with legal restrictions linked to the 'legitimacy' of residence and citizenship.

While housing vulnerability may be a permanent lifelong experience for some, the risk of vulnerability is more typically a transient condition coinciding with transitional stages in an individual's life course. These transitions are particularly related to changes in educational status, employment status and marital status. They occur at different chronological ages related, for example, to the age of leaving full-time education, entry to the labour market, first marriage, birth of first child, and exit from the labour market. Transition stages are the key decision points in an individual's life at which choices are made which determine (or at least affect) future life circumstances. The degree to which choices are constrained at the transition stages (by low educational attainment, employment status or marital status) influence the later life course choices. The youth stage is critical in this respect and it is significant that legislation in some countries reflects the increasing difficulties of youth to adult transition by the imposition, for example, of age eligibility criteria for access to certain benefits. The importance of housing in these life course transitions will vary between the youth, adult and old age stages. In the youth stage, housing plays a subordinate role to choices related to educational, employment and relationship issues. In adulthood and old age the importance of housing is dependent on family status and residential choice is shaped by household requirements and employment status. The role of the family and of social relations and (informal and formal) support will also differ. Transition stages can also be conceived as points of disruption which may fracture an

coping strategy especially if this is linked to a period of
person's life. The transition stage is linked to a shift in the
individual in relation to education, employment or family status.
the stress of transition can also lead to loss of employment, relationship
down or loss of a home.

In summary, housing vulnerability among Europe's population is the creation
of complex interactions between economic and social structures which have
undergone cumulative change during the last quarter of the 20th century. This
change has impacted significantly on the configuration of the labour force, the
operation of the housing market and on social relationships. The transition
from Fordism to post-Fordism has fragmented the inherited and traditional
divisions of a workforce created in an era of industrialisation, and replaced it
with one based on the concept of flexibility, leading to increased job insecurity,
low pay and long-term unemployment among some sectors of the population.
Those households caught up in this process of flexibilisation have been exposed
to an increased risk of housing vulnerability as the housing market, itself
responding to post-Fordist influences, has (re)commodified. Access to housing
across Europe is increasingly determined solely on the basis of financial criteria;
financial insecurity and housing vulnerability go hand in hand. Against this
background, the condition of housing vulnerability has also been significantly
aggravated for those who have lost out (perhaps only temporarily) in the
reshaping of European social formations. Of the multifarious social and
demographic changes that have impacted on Europe in recent decades, the
fragmentation of the traditional nuclear family and the development of a range
of household types which lack economic and social stability has been, perhaps,
the most significant. For the young (when they leave home, particularly if they
have few job skills and low educational attainment), for some older households
(following retirement and its associated financial difficulties) and for those
(particularly women) who experience family break-up during adulthood
(through divorce, separation or as a consequence of domestic violence), housing
vulnerability has become an inexorable part of life experience.

Amid all these changes which have led to the creation of new vulnerabilities,
many continue to experience housing vulnerability today as in the past as a
consequence of social stigma. We are referring here to those who suffer the
indignity of discrimination as a consequence of race, immigrant status or disability.
The recent heightened levels of anti-immigrant prejudices, expressed through
the increasingly vociferous and politically influential parties of the new right,
bear witness, in particular, to the continuing vulnerability of people who are
judged to have no legitimate right of residence in the nations of Europe (Walker,
2002)[1].

Beyond the market and the state

The inability of the private market and the contracting and fragmenting social
sector to cater for the housing needs of those on the margins has obliged many

who experience housing vulnerability to fall back on more informal channels of access and support. Alternative housing provision, outside the formal market and the state, sometimes takes quite dramatic forms, such as in the 'shanty towns' of Portugal. Less dramatically, such provision is apparent, for example, in the 'rented mattresses syndromes' in the immigrant areas of some northern inner cities. As will be demonstrated later in this chapter, the securing of at least basic shelter in such 'housing of last resort' is a material manifestation of 'coping strategies' which are often forced on vulnerable households as the only alternative to homelessness. Such coping strategies, even those which result in shanty town development or mattress renting, are rooted, for the most part (though not always), in the pre-existence of strong community ties in which social cohesiveness is characterised by a 'stock' of social capital and in which reciprocal arrangements are pervasive.

Social capital, social cohesion and reciprocity

The character of a cohesive society is determined by the nature of the social relationships between individuals who comprise that society. It is through these links and relationships that people build up a stock of social capital (Bourdieu, 1985). Social capital is a distinctive form of capital, separate from, but linked to, economic capital and cultural capital (Holt-Jensen, 2000)[2]. Economic capital refers to financial assets, which are generally provided by income from work. It is precisely this kind of capital that is most often absent among those experiencing housing vulnerability. Cultural capital refers to belief and value systems, and the development of a sense of belonging. This latter aspect is closely related to social capital which has been defined as

> ... the sum of resources accruing to an individual by virtue of being enmeshed in networks of more or less institutionalised relationships of mutual acquaintance and recognition, or through membership of a group. (Waquant, 1998, quoted in Holt-Jensen, 2000, p 9)

Holt-Jensen argues that it is possible to distinguish between informal social capital – shifting social ties based on exchange, trust and obligations – and formal social capital – relationships "anchored in formal organisations in which the individual participates as a member or client" (Holt-Jensen, 2000, p 9). Fukuyama (1999, p 16) draws these strands together in a more general definition of social capital as "a set of informal values and norms shared among members of a group that permits co-operation among them" for their mutual benefit. Unlike the possession of money (economic capital) or education (part of cultural capital), the acquisition of social capital does not inhere in the individual (Hannan, 2000). It is instead a product of 'embeddedness', a product of an individual's relationships with others. Social capital refers both to the relations, networks and obligations existing in social situations as well as to the product of these interactions (Wall et al, 1998). On the basis of this definition, social capital encompasses social participation, social networks and social support, all reflecting strong reciprocity. The 'stock' or strength of social capital, it is argued, determines the degree or level of social cohesion in a community.

Social capital manifests itself in different ways in different communities. In deprived areas where housing vulnerability is a demonstrable feature of the environment, close family ties, mutual aid and voluntarism often figure strongly, and it is this social capital, and the reciprocity associated with it, which enables people to cope with poverty, unemployment and poor housing conditions. For example, Pahl (1984) showed, in a study of redundancy among the population of the Isle of Sheppey to the east of London, that a job provides people not only with financial earnings, but also with connections in social networks which serve as gateways to mutual aid and other forms of support, including housing support. From the same perspective, Hannan (2000) demonstrates that a person's social network is a significant factor in whether unemployed people are able to find a job. Her research suggests that who people know, how they know them, and the consequences for differing relationships in people's lives are important components in explaining successful labour market and (we can argue) housing (re)insertion. Social relations are a key determinant in successfully keeping people in their place of residence and in shaping an individual's opportunities in the housing market. However, social networks and social support do more than provide an individual with practical or instrumental support. At a basic level, social relations help individuals to develop their sense of self and their expectation about the world and hence their efficacy and competence in realising 'life choices'. A socially cohesive community is one in which social capital ensures not only community support for vulnerable individuals, but also nourishes independent and proactive involvement on the part of vulnerable people themselves[3]. Social cohesiveness characterises those communities in which housing vulnerability can be mollified through engagement with coping strategies which call on supportive social relationships embedded in reciprocity.

The social cohesion of communities across Europe, and the stock of social capital on which that cohesion depends, have been sorely tested over recent times. Associational relations based around work related activities, for example, have been shattered by the widespread process of deindustrialisation consequent on the competitive impact of globalisation, leading to an undermining of social relations in industrial localities and the break-up of 'traditional' communities. Community reciprocity, based on social relations cultivated through the workplace, has been eroded, and together with the fragmentation of social networks threaten the very bonds of support which provide the basis for social cohesion, thereby increasing the risk of and exposure to housing vulnerability. The erosion of social cohesiveness has been further advanced by socio-demographic change which, in some communities, is symbiotically related to the destruction of the workplace.

The waning of the traditional family, in its extended and nuclear manifestations, and its replacement by more vulnerable household formations has, it is claimed (see, for example, Putnam, 2000), damaged an important part of the social formation which underpinned social relations and the stock of social capital in communities across Europe. The present-day debate about the impact of these economic and demographic changes echo some of the arguments about the disappearance of 'mechanical solidarity' (Durkheim, 1984) and *Gemeinschaft* (Tönnies, 1955) associated with 19th century industrialisation and urbanisation. Just as these earlier disputes, while clearly identifying real social change, exaggerated the longer term effects, so current arguments – while again identifying a real process of change which has immediate corrosive effects on some present day communities – might well be exaggerating the long-term impacts. Detailed research on the nature of social networks in poor neighbourhoods points to the importance of even weak social links – what Henning and Leiberg (1996, p 6) refer to as "unpretentious everyday contacts" – in sustaining vulnerable and marginal groups (see also Kesteloot and Meert, 1999).

The relatively recent engagement by many central and local governments and indeed, as we have seen by the EU itself (see Chapter Two of this volume), with issues of social exclusion testifies to the increasing importance the concepts of social cohesion and social capital have in the development of a European social agenda. A raft of national and local social programmes enacted over recent decades provide clear evidence of government reliance – for the success of their policies – on the existence of community solidarity and cohesion; a presumption of reciprocity lies at the heart of many such initiatives. In Britain, for example, a central concern of the neighbourhood renewal strategy has been that neighbourhood decline is associated with a reduction in social solidarity and social order; population turnover erodes familiarity and trust with a consequent decline in social capital. Lack of progress in previous urban regeneration strategies, it is now recognised, lay with the failure to acknowledge this and to address its absence. Neighbourhood decline policies and initiatives were never going to be successful when implemented in a climate of community disengagement and disillusionment. The absence of cohesion, social capital and reciprocity from many, especially the most deprived communities, is now capturing the attention of government and stimulating the development of initiatives designed to (re)create community. Today, the concepts of cohesion, social capital and reciprocity appear in a wide variety of policy discourses, ranging from the EU programmes (for example, 'Urban' in the case of deprived neighbourhoods in European cities, 'Leader+' to install different forms of partnerships and social networks in a socially fragmented countryside) to nostalgic discussions at the local level, dealing, for example, with the necessity to restore community feelings within a neighbourhood.

The stock of social capital and of social cohesiveness in a community is also of considerable importance for the success of what we might label the strategy or tactic of '*re*familialisation', presently being pursued by many European governments. This policy is a direct reversal of the *de*familialisation process, whereby the welfare state, in its heyday, took to itself the caring role traditionally performed in families and communities (see Esping-Andersen, 1999; Sainsbury, 1996). The most overt example of this strategy is the initiation of de-institutionalisation and care in the community programmes in several European countries (see Edgar et al, 2000, pp 33-68) which actively encourage the transfer of responsibility for the welfare needs of dependent people back into the communities from which they came. In practice this often means the adoption of support responsibilities by the immediate family of the dependent person. In a context in which some family households are beset with job insecurity and housing vulnerability and in which some communities are experiencing an erosion of social cohesiveness and of social capital, the chances of success for such a strategy is diminished. More generally, the process of refamilialisation is to be seen in the encouragement and promotion of community self-help and empowerment programmes. These strategies can be seen as a further manifestation of the process of the 'hollowing out' of state functions and responsibilities – a devolving of welfare and care responsibilities to non-state or quasi-state organisations (community councils, tenant groups and so on). Such strategies in their turn can be seen as a further example of retrenchment of welfare.

In the Fordist period, the perverse effects of market exchange were mainly tempered by state redistribution, leading in some instances to the 'redundancy' of many social networks and reciprocal arrangements – a process of defamilialisation (De Decker and Meert, 2000). Nowadays, as the redistributive sphere plays a more modest role in tempering market disadvantages, a greater role is reserved for the reciprocal arrangements, in which partnerships and voluntary work play a significant part.

Low-income groups and coping strategies in the European housing market

Chapter Three and Four considered some basic macro-social trends and their impact on access to housing for marginalised and low-income groups. However, households, whether affluent or not, should not be seen exclusively as passive human beings reacting deterministically to macro-social processes. There is a dialectical interaction between the micro (the individual or household) and the macro (social structures and processes). Coping strategies adopted by low-income households in the European housing arena clearly demonstrate the complexity of this interrelationship between 'structures', operating at the meso and macro scales, and 'agents', operating predominantly at the micro scale.

In this analysis, coping or survival strategies can be seen as referring to the way individuals or households engage with macro-social obstacles that obstruct their intentions and goals[4]. Such coping strategies often have a clear economic dimension in that they are designed primarily to save money (for example, by minimising housing costs), to earn extra money (for example, by subletting rooms), or to replace market exchange by non-monetarist activities (for example, living with relatives) in order to survive. Here we assess the way vulnerable people, who are unable to gain access to adequate housing through the privatised housing market or through public allocation systems, cope with ongoing exclusionary processes. We focus on those coping strategies that are clearly embedded in small-scale communities and are characterised by reciprocal arrangements. This does not mean that strategies that entail market principles, such as the renting of a mattress, are excluded. On the contrary, it is a challenging idea to assess the extent to which often-romanticised reciprocal arrangements among small-scale communities are affected by the process of commodification.

The following overview focuses on strategies that contribute to the emergence of new settlement patterns and are embedded in at least a gloss of community support[5]. First, by focusing on some examples which can be grouped together with poverty and social exclusion, the broad range of often concealed and therefore highly informal strategies low-income households deploy in order to obtain at least a minimum shelter are outlined. Second, these strategies are discussed in terms of their integrating and/or excluding effect for the concerned households. It will become clear that many strategies are strongly related with similar – and mostly informal – strategies in the labour intensive segments of the job market.

Coping strategies and the creation of informal settlements

The Portuguese shanty towns around the metropolitan areas of Porto and Lisbon provided, until recently, perhaps the most dramatic and oldest examples of informal settlements in the EU. The recently initiated Programma Especial de Realojamento (PER), however, aims to rehouse the tens of thousand of dwellers in these shanty towns, though present progress with the project is slow. New shanty towns have emerged very recently elsewhere in the EU. In Greece, for instance, about 45,000 people, mainly gypsies, survive in tents, caravans, containers and other substitute dwellings (Sapounakis, 2001). The dominating public discourse on these gypsy settlements implicitly refers to the community tradition of these people, their nomadic way of life and their strong social networks. This is used to justify the Greek state's non-intervention strategy and its reluctance to support them in finding access to the better segments of the housing market. However, representatives of the gypsies in Greece clearly reject this politically naive interpretation. They refer to their structural deprivation in the labour market, the housing market and within the education system. Their complete neglect by public authorities (some municipalities now try to collaborate in order to fight the most extreme forms of deprivation among the gypsies) stands in contrast to the welcome the Greek state extends towards the expatriates from Pontos (ex-USSR), for whom 6,500 new dwellings were erected by the end of 2000.

Coping strategies which involve the use of informal housing embedded in collective settlements and reciprocal arrangements are not exclusive to the southern European welfare states. An examination of countries elsewhere in the EU, reveals the existence and ongoing reproduction of a variety of informal housing situations, which, taken altogether, can be seen as the result of a dialectical interplay between macro-structural trends and individual or household coping strategies, in which the outcome is a high share of home ownership with clear reciprocal support.

In France the phenomenon of shanty towns is generally only discussed as an historical occurrence, for instance in reference to the well-known Algerian bidonvilles of Nanterres or the barracks of the Portuguese in Champigny (see Sayad, 1995; Volovitch-Tavares, 1995). The fact that many of the former French shanty towns were finally replaced by multi-storey public housing complexes (HLM) symbolised the strengthening of the decommodifying process within the French welfare state during the 1960s and the following decades. However, within the present context of new waves of labour migrants and asylum seekers, the French welfare state seems to reflect the same shortcomings as in the early 1950s when thousands of Algerian and other immigrants settled down in a wide range of shanty towns around the major metropolitan areas of France. Indeed, nowadays the number of Roma gypsies, settling down on new shanty towns around Paris, is rapidly increasing. In Choisy-le-Roi, Vitry and Orly, three municipalities in the Marne valley south of Paris, many hundreds of Roma gypsies recently established an informal and illegal settlement in the shadow of a busy highway and heavily polluting industry (Carayol, 2002; Meert and Bourgeois, 2002). They cleared ground which in the past served as a dumping site, and then installed rather shoddy caravans and other forms of shelter. Social networks seem to be important in launching and 'promoting' these new shanty towns among the newly arrived Roma gypsies in the metropolitan areas of Paris. More 'developed' welfare states, compared to the formative version of Portugal and Greece, therefore also reflect structural shortcomings towards people such as gypsies who generally lack any form of citizenship. As a consequence, being excluded from the free market (housing and jobs) and the redistribution mechanisms of the state, these people have finally opted for or fallen back on community-based forms of self-help and collective support.

In the Netherlands, despite its widespread and highly organised public housing sector, examples of 'coping strategies' which result in the occupation of a caravan, a mobile home or a boat can also be identified. The 1998 housing survey revealed that 309,000 Dutch households lived in what was called 'other occupied accommodation' (De Feijter, 2001). This segment can be divided into three parts: 117,000 housing units (for example, for students), 74,000 households living in houseboats, caravans and such like, and 46,000 rented rooms in private houses. The households who occupy the caravans, houseboats and other substitute dwellings can be classified in the main as belonging to the targeted group for social housing. The majority of these households are couples (sometimes with children), they are not new households just entering the housing market.

Some of these households in these sites do not have a compelling history of structural deprivation. Inspired by alternative life norms and values, they have deliberately chosen this alternative housing option. Franke (1998), however, has identified a number of complex motivations for seeking shelter in Dutch camping and other recreational grounds. In a first case, he identifies people who, though originally in urgent need of a dwelling (for example, after a divorce), have after a while chosen to live permanently in what was originally conceived of as temporary housing, mostly because it is cheap and quiet. A second motivation is related to restrictions on access presented by locally overpriced and overheated housing markets to which the poorest households respond by purchasing or hiring a caravan, chalet or other substitute dwelling as an escape route. A third kind of motivation can be summarised as realising an old dream of working class members after retirement, that is to own their dwelling in a rural setting (answering the lure of the rural idyll).

In Belgium considerable detailed and qualitative research has been carried out about such types of illegal and informal housing strategies. Focusing on the permanent habitation of camping grounds and other recreational areas, a survey carried out in Flanders during the winter period of 1996-7 (Mens en Ruimte, 1997) revealed that about 11,500 people lived in caravans and other rather shoddy substitute dwellings, while in the Walloon part of the country a survey of 1999 (Fondation Roi Baudouin, 1999) counted more than 9,000 dwellers (undoubtedly a serious underestimation due to administrative restrictions on the available data). In the Flemish survey, the effects of the disintegration of the labour market are illustrated by the fact that only one fifth of those interviewed were part of a household in which at least one member was employed. About one third of the respondents were unemployed, 15% were ill or disabled, and the remainder were retired. In half the cases the educational background of the respondent was limited to primary school. The main income for almost 80% of the interviewed population consisted of welfare allowances (unemployment, illness and retirement). More detailed research results revealed the clear impact of the retrenchment of the welfare state on this population. Their unstable residential history and the lack of a local domicile, which is often the case for the most impoverished among them, caused numerous suspensions of unemployment allowances because people were not accessible for state monitoring. This monitoring was designed to verify whether they were prepared to join the labour market, should an offer of employment be made (Meert, 1998). More than 50% of the respondents reported that they had severe problems subsisting within their available budget. Measuring poverty by using the official Belgian poverty standard, almost 15% were in poverty (the share of households experiencing poverty in Flanders, defined by the same criterion, is 2.1%). These poor socio-economic living conditions are also reflected in the housing conditions of most of the households staying permanently on campsites. More than one third of households live without basic amenities (lack of an indoor toilet, running water or a shower), while only 14% of Flemish households as a whole live in such conditions. More than two fifths of the campsite dwellings have less than 35 square metres of living space, and 75% less than 54 square metres. More than 50% of the households complain of an insufficient number of bedrooms. Frozen water pipes, wet and mouldy walls, inadequate noise insulation are all discomforts that complete the picture. This inferior housing quality corresponds to low basic charges (site charge, plus rent or hire-purchase of the caravan), at least when compared with the average charges paid by a Flemish household.

The rise in permanent occupancy of campsites in Flanders since the early 1990s is intimately linked to the crises on the labour and the housing markets, which is strongly articulated in the deprived 19th-century belts of the larger Belgian cities. The temporary economic prosperity of the second half of the 1980s was followed by a steep rise in housing prices, restricted, at the outset, to the Brussels-Capital Region but later spreading to the whole of Flanders. Undoubtedly, this process has driven many vulnerable households, forced to pay unreasonably high prices on the private urban rental market, to the fringes of the housing market and thus to the campsites. Following this trend, in the largest concentration of campsite dwellers in Flanders (the hamlet of Schiplaken, near the city of Mechelen) nearly 60% of the new inhabitants in 1995 had left the Brussels-Capital Region to settle down in inferior caravans or other basic shelters. Their previous dwellings belonged to the residual rental sector, which dominates the 19th century belt of the city (Meert, 2001).

Several in-depth surveys revealed the existence of strong social networks among the campsite dwellers (see, for example, Bourgeois, 2000; Meert, 2000, 2001). Two aspects should be taken into account to explain this. First of all, mouth-to-mouth promotion is important in making the camping sites known as a potential location of cheap, alternative housing. This promotion is organised through the social networks of relatives and former neighbours in urban communities. These networks are to a large extent preserved when the 'linked' households live together on the campsites. Second, the fact of living together, in a context of informality and illegality, also contributes to a common set of interests which strengthens mutual solidarity and social networks.

Even in Denmark, which of all the EU countries has the best developed welfare state facilities, unusual and illegal housing – consisting of self-built constructions or discarded replacement shelters built in the vicinity of garbage dumps or along the outfall of main sewers – though rare, have existed since the 1930s (Nordgaard and Koch-Nielsen, 2001). In the community of Christiana in Copenhagen about 1000 people live and survive in former army barracks. In contrast to the cited Belgian and Dutch examples, many of these communities are now undergoing a process of gentrification, with an increasing proportion of people with better education and higher incomes. Alongside the voluntary alternative lifestyle of such affluent households, involving the sale of alternative houses at very high prices, such communities also shelter low-income groups who survive by renting shanty-like barracks and other inferior shelters. From their perspective, the ongoing gentrification process is a threat, leading to increasing rents and even evictions from this informal segment of the Danish housing market.

Coping strategies and the informal housing market

Housing strategies, established within a community context and relying on social networks and reciprocal engagements, are not limited to the very visible settlements such as shanty-towns or permanently inhabited camping sites. In what follows, some more concrete examples of coping strategies in Spain and Belgium are briefly dealt with. These are located within the existing built environment and are symptomatic of the importance of the informal housing market for some sections of the population in the EU.

In the case of Spain, Cabrera (2001) points to the fact that in Madrid, where rental costs are excessive, it is not unusual to find people (especially immigrants) sharing an overcrowded dwelling in which the same bed is rotated through a three-shift system of eight hours each. This phenomenon is known as 'warm bedding'. In particular, the newly arrived Ecuadorians rely on such desperate strategies to find shelter. They sublet rooms individually or in shifts, and hire beds and even sofas by the hour – and this mainly from compatriots who already have their settlement papers in order. These examples reflect the double-sided characteristic of many survival strategies (see for example, Kesteloot and Meert [1999] on the nature of ethnic entrepreneurship). On the one hand, it serves as a strategy to provide the settled Ecuadorian subletters with a surplus income to complement other irregular earnings, such as street vending. On the other hand, it allows their most deprived compatriots to cut their expenditures on housing to a minimum. Taken together, these strategies illustrate that the tight community relations among immigrants, even when their origin of out-migration is identical, should not be too romanticised. Although this informal segment of the Madrid housing market is clearly embedded in the social relations and networks among the Ecuadorian immigrants, in the end the access to the shelter is realised by financial transactions, based on pure market principles. From this perspective, the way the poorest immigrants access housing in urban areas does not differ fundamentally from the way other immigrants are sheltered on the Spanish countryside. Cabrera (2001) refers to a devastating report about the housing situation of many of the more than 40,000 foreign immigrants who live in West Almeria. Nowadays, the great majority (between 60% and 80%) live spread out in the country in small Andalusian farmhouses and storehouses, alongside the greenhouses they work in. Usually, Cabrera states, these are sheds used for storing farming implements, and they cannot be considered as places to accommodate people. They rarely have bathrooms or kitchens, and frequently workers have to live alongside insecticides and animals. Typically they are charged for these places of 'shelter' and the cost is often taken from their wages.

In the case of Belgium, the previously discussed phenomenon of inhabited campsites should not overshadow the wide-scale existence of the so-called inner-city slums in which, similar to the Spanish experience, many low-income groups live and survive, in a close relationship with the informal labour market. A recent Flemish overview of a diverse range of substitute dwellings, such as caravans, garage boxes, barns, vans, but also more classical types of inadequate and substandard housing, revealed the importance of what can be readily called the inner-city slums (Meert et al, 2002). In particular, in the 19th century belts of big cities such as Ghent, Antwerp and Brussels, many thousands of low-income households (mainly immigrants, but also older Belgian, mostly single households) dwell in rented rooms without a written contract. They lack basic amenities and experience insecure housing conditions; some have tried to escape from these marginal housing conditions by leasing or purchasing a caravan or substitute dwelling in a more rural context (De Decker, 1994).

The social reproduction of homelessness, reciprocal arrangements and survival strategies

The above examples make clear that the variety of household survival strategies in the private housing market is clearly linked to the omnipresence of social exclusion and poverty in the EU. People trying to survive in illegally inhabited and purchased Dutch caravans, in illegally sublet Spanish rooms or in redundant barracks have very limited opportunities for upward social mobility. These consciously executed coping strategies associated with the informal and unregulated end of the housing market, while providing rudimentary shelter, contribute at the same time to the (re)production of the most inferior segments of the private housing market. As such, it is clear that these small-scale and often individually deployed coping strategies have a very limited capacity to induce changes in the underlying structural determinants of capitalist society, such as the juxtaposition of extreme poverty and wealth. In order to influence these underlying structures, more collective forms of organisations are needed if the structures of social inequality are to be replaced by those based on concepts of social justice.

However, the verdict of these coping strategies should not be too severe and negative. Qualitative surveys among Danish and Flemish cases (Sørensen, 1993; Meert et al, 1997; Bourgeois, 2000) reveal that shanty town-like areas have stronger social networks than other deprived neighbourhoods. This inspires policy makers to formalise to some extent the neighbourhoods that rely on these informal household strategies. Although this orientation deserves a lot of credit, it might encourage a downgrading and erosion of housing-related state intervention. Of course, in the case of the Portuguese shanty towns of Lisbon and Porto, there is no defensible alternative than to get rid of them and to rehouse the more than 130,000 families (Bruto da Costa and Bapatista, 2001) who lived through generations in such areas.

In contrast to the Portuguese approach, the Danish official housing initiative of Unusual Dwellings to Unusual Characters, launched in 1998, wants to respect as much as possible the alternative lifestyles of the inhabitants of informal housing (Nordgaard and Koch-Nielsen, 2001), even if a large proportion of the inhabitants live in poverty. Although in some cases, municipalities seem to overestimate the social capacity of networks among the dwellers of caravans, army barracks and other substitute dwellings by concluding that social assistance is not needed in these areas (Nordgaard and Koch-Nielsen, 2001, p 53), this Danish initiative merits attention. The initiative was initially designed to run over a four-year period and a fund was set up to which local innovators could apply for support. From 2001 the initiative has been made permanent and integrated in the Social Housing Act. One of the projects in Copenhagen is highly innovative. It is an 'Illu-housing project' for Greenlanders who, according to research, like to be close to the sea and to sleep in the open. The plan is to locate the Illu-housing in the southern harbour of Copenhagen and to involve Greenlanders in the construction of their own houses. Literally, the plan is that the ordinary installations like a toilet and a kitchen are constructed by formal artisans, while Greenlanders can construct the rest of the house themselves, with the municipality paying for the materials (Nordgaard and Koch-Nielsen, 2001, p 54). Such self-help projects are clearly closely related to policies designed to empower vulnerable individuals in seeking a solution to their own predicament.

In Belgium, the Flemish government has similar objectives with regard to the rehousing of campsite dwellers, which in fact boils down to a formalisation of informally developed housing strategies. In a pioneering municipality, a project has been launched to build dozens of specifically designed brick houses, which reflect, in their style and minimal comfort, the form and conditions of a caravan (Meert, 2000). The very limited floor area (a net surface of 55 square metres) means that this programme will introduce the smallest dwellings ever supplied by the social housing sector in Belgium. The motivation for this policy comes from the expressions of satisfaction that most campsite dwellers proudly express when they are interviewed about their housing situations and their wholly owned dwelling in a green surrounding. However, most of these cursorily organised inquiries do not demonstrate the profound problems that come to the surface during in-depth interviews. As such, the formalisation of informal housing strategies, often relying on perverse market-related situations of exploitation, raise questions with ambiguous answers for the policy that has to be pursued.

Notes

[1] The issue of homelessness and immigration forms the subject matter of the fifth book in this series, due for publication in 2003.

[2] The concepts of social capital, social cohesion and reciprocity are very fashionable today, but they are not new concepts. Reciprocity, for example, was discussed by Mauss in the 1920s, while social capital was dealt with by Silverman in the 1930s. See Svendsen and Svendsen (2000) and Falk and Kilpatrick (2000).

[3] However, social relations, and the stock of social capital these relations reflect, cannot be isolated from the social context in which they operate. As Kearns and Forrest (2000, p 1011) conclude," a high degree of mutual and voluntary activity in a neighbourhood

lacking key economic resources of jobs and incomes will produce quite different outcomes compared with similarly observed activities in an affluent area". The presence of a strong social capital and a high degree of social cohesion cannot be assumed, in every circumstance, to be a natural good since strong socially cohesive groups can be exclusive and disabling as well as supportive and enabling. Cities can consist of socially cohesive but increasingly divided neighbourhoods (for example, Belfast).

[4] The concept of coping or survival 'strategies' has been extensively discussed in the sociological literature (Crow, 1989; Morgan, 1989; Mingione, 1991; Anderson et al, 1994).

[5] Such strategies should not be confused with the practises of new age travellers and other voluntarily selected lifestyles, which go hand in hand with the permanent inhabiting of mobile homes and other unusual 'dwellings'.

SIX

Access to housing and the European social agenda

Introduction

The European social agenda, agreed at Nice in December 2000, recognised the role of social policy as a key instrument in the reduction of inequalities and promotion of social cohesion. Following the addition of the fight against exclusion among the social policy provisions of the Treaty of Amsterdam (articles 136 and 137), the European Council of Lisbon agreed the need to take steps to make a decisive impact on the eradication of poverty by 2010. It also agreed that member states' policies for combating social exclusion should be based on an open method of coordination combining common objectives, National Action Plans (NAPs), and a programme presented by the European Commission (EC) to encourage cooperation in this field. In the synthesis report submitted to the European Council of Stockholm in 2001, the EC began an assessment of policy strategies and policy outcomes in four key interlinked domains: economic reform, information society, internal market, and social cohesion. The significance of this decision for the analysis of this volume is that, for the first time, housing and homelessness issues were introduced into the debate on the European social agenda.

The joint report on social inclusion drawing on the National Action Plans and presented to the Council and the European Parliament identifies eight core challenges (EC, 2001). One of these challenges is defined as ensuring good accommodation for all. In all countries this requires action to prevent and address homelessness. In some countries, it means developing appropriate integrated responses to homelessness for the first time. It also means dealing with excluded places, as well as excluded people, through the regeneration of areas of multiple deprivation.

In agreeing the European social agenda at Nice, the member states agreed to develop their National Action Plans on Social Inclusion (NAPs/incl) within the framework of four common objectives. These objectives develop from the First Report on Economic and Social Cohesion which conceived the European social model to be based on a social market economy combined with elements of social solidarity (EC, 1996). Social cohesion, in this context, is perceived in terms of reduction in social and economic disparities and open access to services of general benefit and protection. The objectives are summarised as:

1. facilitating participation in employment and access by all to resources, rights, goods and services;
2. preventing the risks of exclusion;
3. helping the most vulnerable;
4. mobilising all relevant actors.

These four objectives have very specific implications for access to housing for vulnerable groups and for homeless people. The objective to facilitate participation in employment identifies "for those most vulnerable in society, pathways towards employment by mobilising training policies" (EC, 2001, p 32). This implies the integration of homeless services and employment training services. The objective of facilitating access to resources and rights specifically refers to the need to implement policies to "provide access for all to decent and sanitary housing" (EC, 2001, p 40). The objective of preventing the risks of social exclusion also refers explicitly to the need for policies to prevent life crises which can lead to situations of social exclusion such as "indebtedness ... and becoming homeless" (p 60). The objective of helping the most vulnerable refers to those who belong to a "group experiencing integration problems" (p 68) and to those who live in "areas marked by exclusion". The final objective – to mobilise all relevant actors – refers to the need for 'joined-up policies' and therefore to the horizontal integration of activities designed to deal with these problems. It also implies the need to improve institutional coordination and inter-agency working.

This chapter considers the approaches used to tackle housing exclusion in the EU member states in relation to these common objectives.

Spatial scale and social exclusion

The EU programme to combat poverty and social exclusion has been established within the framework of a "new open method of coordination" (EC, 2000). The development of NAPs/incl based on a common set of objectives and the development of comparable indicators provides (potentially) the framework for promoting the exchange of good practice and mutual learning at European Community level, and should encourage integration and coordination within countries. This feature of coordination refers to what may be called 'horizontal integration' – coordination and partnership between institutions and stakeholders. However, the NAPs will be ineffective if they do not link national policies and programmes to the neighbourhood level where homelessness and disadvantage occur. Hence, vertical integration is also important in linking policies at the European, national, regional, municipal and local scales. The summary report on the National Action Plans (EC, 2001), as well as recognising the need to regenerate areas of multiple deprivation, refers specifically to this challenge of vertical integration in relation to the improvement of service delivery. There is reference first to the need to complement NAPs with integrated approaches at regional and local level. Second, there is recognition of the need to address the issue of the links between the national, regional and local levels particularly in those member states with strong regional (or federal) structures.

It has been argued that "it is access to decision making, access to resources and access to common narratives" (Madanipour, 1998, p 80) which enable social integration. Throughout our analysis so far we have examined the production of housing vulnerability and homelessness in relation to the factors of the market, governance and civil society. However, Madanipour also argues that "many of these forms of access have clear spatial manifestations, as space is the site in which these different forms of access are made possible or denied" (1998, p 80). Therefore, strategies for tackling housing exclusion should reflect this spatial dimension. In this context, we would highlight three principles that should underpin strategies to tackle housing exclusion and homelessness.

First, we can distinguish different layers of space resulting from historical investment patterns and the differential impact of economic restructuring. The impact of such structural change will vary from locality to locality. Hence policies to prevent or address homelessness must take account of variations in local economic and housing market contexts. Homelessness strategies need to be developed for the local level in order to inform national priorities and policies.

Second, some localities are richer than others in terms of institutional capacity and institutional networks (Amin and Thrift, 1995; Obsourne, 1998). The importance of the voluntary sector in service provision for vulnerable and homeless people – and the impact of changing financial and regulatory relationships – is well known. It is arguable that the distribution of institutional capacity developed by historical voluntary action, influenced by public sector funding priorities, does not correspond exactly to changing and emerging patterns of need. There will therefore inevitably be a need to develop additional capacity in particular areas. This may involve strategies both to strengthen local networks of agencies to ensure that they pay attention to housing exclusion, or it may require the creation of new agencies at the local level by mobilising and empowering local stakeholders. It should also involve empowerment of individuals and community groups through engagement in local action and decision-making structures.

Third, the multidimensional nature of social exclusion finds spatial manifestation in geographical concentrations of poverty and disadvantage which have persisted and are in fact worsening (Glennerster et al, 1999). The visible social polarisation evidenced by concentrations of disadvantaged people in particular parts of most European cities creates "disconnected places" (Forrest, 2000, p 207). The nature of urban regeneration policies, designed to tackle areas of multiple deprivation, has been criticised for lacking a strategic approach (MacGregor and McConnachie, 1995) and for being dominated by considerations of land and property rather than community (Madanipour, 1998). Such policies have therefore exacerbated exclusionary processes of the property market rather than combated them. This has occurred through gentrification processes, through the eradication of low-cost lodging houses and cheap, if poor quality, housing

(De Feijter, 2000) as well as by changing allocation and management processes on difficult-to-let social housing estates (Vestergaard, 1998). Hence, strategies to tackle housing exclusion need to be focussed on community regeneration, implying a focusing of integration of policy action at the local or neighbourhood level. These principles provide a context within which strategies to tackle housing exclusion should be set. The remainder of this chapter examines examples of strategies to tackle housing exclusion in relation to the key objectives established to tackle poverty and social exclusion in Europe.

Strategies for tackling housing exclusion

This section considers strategies for tackling housing exclusion in the framework of the four objectives of the European social agenda. Using these objectives we identify five main approaches to tackling housing exclusion and examples of distinctive strategies within each objective. These are:

1. *Facilitating access to resources, rights, goods and services for all*
i.   legislation regarding rights of access to housing;
ii.   strategies for provision of housing for vulnerable groups;
iii. guaranteeing affordable housing for vulnerable and low-income people.

2. *Facilitating participation in employment*
i.   training programmes;
ii.   integration of employment and resettlement initiatives.

3. *Preventing the risks of exclusion*
i.   implementation of homelessness strategies;
ii.   prevention of eviction;
iii. maintaining tenancies in the rental housing market.

4. *Helping the most vulnerable*
i.   support and housing;
ii.   supporting specific vulnerable groups;
iii. action in areas marked by exclusion.

5. *Mobilising all relevant bodies*
i.   coordination of action;
ii.   local partnership examples;
iii. multi-agency working.

In discussing each of these strategies, examples have been chosen to illustrate the issues involved. It is not intended to imply that these approaches are typical of the overall approach to homelessness in particular countries.

Facilitating access to housing

Chapter Two discussed the issue of the right to housing and examined the nature of this right at the international, EU and national level. In this section we examine recent changes in the legislative framework in relation to the specification of vulnerable groups and recognition of the rights or needs of the homeless.

Legislation regarding rights of access to housing

Belgium and France have specific laws formulated in part around the concept of the right to housing. Since 1994, Belgium has constitutionally recognised the right to decent housing. The regional legislators of Flanders and Wallonia have taken over the principle of housing right in their legislation; the Brussels-Capital Region did not. In both Wallonia and Flanders, the promotion of a better quality of housing is linked to the realisation of the promotion of housing right as being a basic social right. However, legislation is only as good as its implementation. Although a wide range of instruments is now available, compared to the number of housing market transactions and the amount of money involved in the housing sector, governmental impetus is rather modest. In this regard it is important to stress that roofless and houseless people very rarely pass through to social renting. Indeed, despite the constitutional right to decent housing, homeless people are (with the exception of those in Wallonia) not accepted as a priority group. As a consequence, long waiting times (several years) push them to the private rental sector, which rarely provides adequate or affordable accommodation.

The *Loi Besson* in France is intended to guarantee access to decent housing for low-income groups. As a consequence of the *Loi Besson*, new institutions appeared in France (mainly on a local scale) to offer low-budget dwellings and especially to create initiatives facilitating access to decent housing – for example real estate agencies with social objectives (*agencies immobilières à vocation sociale*). Four main mechanisms have been employed to enlarge the supply of low-budget dwellings for vulnerable groups:

1 opening up existing markets (for example, by tax exemption when dwellings will be rented to low-income households);
2 encouraging ownership (for example, supplementary taxes on vacant dwellings);
3 the production of social and 'very' social rented houses;
4 the provision of emergency shelters and temporary accommodation.

Four social categories are identified as the most vulnerable on the housing market: single parents, large families, foreigners, and young people. The Fonds de Solidarite Logement (FSL) mainly assists single adults and single parents. This fund should have been sufficient to assist 230,000 households in 1998.

However, the whole range of measures to facilitate access had a very limited impact. The 1% housing fund is now mainly used to assist young people. This money is mainly managed and distributed by third sector agencies paying guarantees and deposits (€1.4 million in 1998). Meanwhile, 12,500 beds have been added to the existing infrastructure of emergency shelters between 1993 and 2000. This seems to be an important decision, as the demand for this infrastructure is growing because of the lack of alternatives for the homeless.

The UK and Ireland both have legislation that focuses specifically on homelessness. Recent legislation in England (the Homelessness Act, 2002) and in Scotland (The Housing Scotland Act, 2001) have extended the duties of local authorities in respect of homelessness and the categories of people eligible for assistance. The Scottish legislation is the most radical and abolishes the distinction between priority and non-priority need in respect of local authorities' duty to ensure the provision of temporary accommodation for homeless people. This means that non-priority homeless people will now for the first time have to be provided with temporary accommodation. This will include single people (that is, those aged 18 and over who are not defined as vulnerable in the 1987 Homelessness Act), childless couples and adult families. This change is significant given the substantial increase in the number of young single people applying for accommodation. While there have been a number of ad hoc initiatives to try to meet this need (for example, additional capital allocations, the Rough Sleepers Initiative) the needs of this group have, until now, been inadequately met. It has been argued (Gill, 2001) that this new duty to provide at least temporary accommodation for (among others) all homeless single people will result in a more thorough assessment of their needs. This is likely since the provision of temporary accommodation will require authorities to come to terms with difficult support and management issues.

The Scottish legislation additionally makes it a statutory duty on housing associations to provide either temporary or permanent accommodation for a homeless person referred to them by a local authority (unless there is good reason not to do so). This is a necessary requirement, since there has been a steady reduction in local authority housing through the right-to-buy and transfers to housing associations. There is no such requirement, however, in the English homelessness legislation which, in other respects, makes similar provisions (for example, the requirement for local authorities to prepare a homelessness strategy). The English legislation also extends the categories of priority need (under regulations) to include homeless 16- to 17-year-olds, care leavers aged 18 to 21, people vulnerable as a result of an institutionalised care background, and people fleeing violence (or the threat of violence).

In Austria, Germany and Luxembourg housing rights are referenced in various strands of national legislation. In Germany, the 2nd Housing Construction Act defines 'priority areas' for public funding and some priority target groups for publicly funded housing (section 26). These target groups include pregnant women, families with children, young couples, single parents with children, the elderly and severely disabled persons. Homeless people are not mentioned.

The legal situation changed considerably in 2002 when new legislation replaced the 2nd Housing Construction Act. In the new Act (*Wohnraumförderungsgesetz* [WoFG]) the aim of state support for the housing needs of 'broad strata of the population' is explicitly dropped. Section 1 of the Bill states that the main target group of support is "households which are not able to procure decent housing by themselves and are in need of support". The same section also specifies target groups for the support of rented housing. Apart from the groups already mentioned above, and "households with low incomes", explicit reference is made to "homeless persons and other persons in need of support" (BMVBW, 2001a). Households threatened by homelessness and households living in unacceptable housing conditions are mentioned as examples for "other persons in need of support" (BMVBW, 2001b, p 34).

Strategies for provision of affordable housing for vulnerable groups

In Finland, the programme to reduce homelessness was drawn up after consultation on housing policy (2002-3). This strategy states unequivocally that "the reduction of homelessness can most effectively be influenced by public housing policies" (Ministry of the Environment, 2001, p 6). The precondition for this is "the co-operation of the state, municipalities, public housing producers and owners of real estate to produce more reasonably priced rented apartments" (2001, p 6). The programme accepts that municipalities have a central role in the reduction of homelessness and proposes that allocation of building land should require the assignment of a proportion of apartments (or whole sites) to meet the needs of homeless households. In addition the subsidies paid from the Finnish Housing Fund to housing associations as "capital subsidies" is to be increased from €3.4 million to €8.4 million between 2002 and 2005. At the same time the subsidy for the acquisition of housing is to be raised from €4,250 to €10,000 per homeless person in Helsinki and to €8,500 elsewhere. The strategy requires the use of acquisition loans, even in a situation of high house prices; this is justified on the grounds that it is a quicker method of reducing homelessness than new construction. Funds are also to be made available, for the first time, to renovate and convert institutional buildings to supported housing. The strategy proposes to use lottery funding for the acquisition of service and support apartments for homeless people with multiple social problems (people with mental health problems and drug addiction are referred to specifically). In combination this programme for the reduction of homelessness will, if successfully implemented, realise over 1000 apartments per year until 2005.

In Ireland, the primary solution has also been to increase the supply of housing. Ireland presently has one of the lowest stocks of housing in Europe per 1,000 of the population – despite record levels of housing construction in recent years. The Planning and Development Act 2000 gives each planning authority the responsibility to prepare a housing strategy within one year of the Act. The objective of the strategy is to 'provide affordable housing' to eligible persons. Eligibility is defined as people in need of accommodation whose income is inadequate for a mortgage because payment would exceed 35% of annual income. Under the provisions of the Act, up to 20% of development land is to be made available by house builders to the local authority for "social and affordable" housing as a condition of planning permission. The council would purchase this land at agricultural use value rather than at market prices for development land. The report of the commission on the private rented residential sector considered tax incentives necessary to stimulate investment in the private rented sector. The government response has been to establish the private rented sector Tenancy Board to rule on disputes between tenants and landlords. However, the Finance Act 2001 brought into operation tax concessions to private renting landlords, including a 'living over the shop scheme' to stimulate the use of underused space.

Facilitating participation in employment

We have argued in earlier chapters that the causes of homelessness and vulnerability in the housing market are the result of a complex interplay of structural and agency factors. Labour market exclusion and flexible labour markets, leading to insecure and low-paid employment and higher levels of unemployment, create the structural conditions for housing market exclusion (see Chapter Three of this volume). Low educational attainment, unstable job histories and low incomes are all factors reported among households experiencing episodes of homelessness. Equally, routes out of homelessness and resettlement strategies are associated with both employment training to improve skills and also with job creation initiatives linked to rehousing projects. It is recognised that vulnerability may be increased among young people at the time of transition from school and entry into the labour market. Foyer projects are a well-known example of attempts to deal with this aspect of housing vulnerability. Some people experience extreme marginalisation from the labour market as a result of a range of personal factors that may include long-term unemployment, illiteracy, behavioural problems resulting from addiction or unusual lifestyles. Specialised training or employment initiatives are appropriate in such circumstances. We have reported in a previous volume (Edgar and Doherty, 2001) that training and employment initiatives for homeless women are exceptional, but are emerging as pilot programmes in some countries (such as Germany).

Employment training programmes

One approach adopted to facilitate participation in employment for vulnerable groups and homeless people is the use of employment training programmes. It has been argued that opportunities for training and employment are often offered to those unemployed people who are seen as being 'more employable', and that more attention should be given to those who have the greatest obstacles to overcome, including hostel residents, people being treated for drug and alcohol dependency, former prisoners and ex-offenders (FEANTSA, 2001). For homeless people in particular, access to training and employment is difficult without access to appropriate accommodation. There are a wide range of examples of projects that provide appropriate accommodation and social support, together with specially adapted training and employment, to facilitate the social reintegration and resettlement of (former) homeless people (see Edgar et al, 1999). However, across Europe there is generally a lack of long-term public funding for such integrated activities.

One example of good practice in the targeting of employment training programmes to the needs of vulnerable households and homeless people has been the Scottish based New Futures Fund (NFF) initiative. This helps to link vulnerable and excluded individuals into appropriate training. Prior to its introduction the government had introduced the New Deal for people who were long-term unemployed, giving them virtually no choice other than to join training for employment. The government recognised that a number of people were not ready for the time-limited New Deal training and set up a 'gateway' to the New Deal, which allowed individuals six months to gain basic literacy skills, and to enable them to take advantage of the New Deal training. The NFF was introduced in May 1998 for the most vulnerable and excluded individuals, who are not ready to enter the 'gateway.' Outcomes which are recognised from the NFF are 'soft' indicators such as increased self-confidence, better family relationships or an ability to work in a team. The funding is used to support organisations who work with excluded people, rather than to traditional training organisations. This encourages socially orientated organisations to include an employment-related element to their work (Aldridge, 2001).

The target groups for the NFF include homeless people, people with addictions, people with mental health problems and people involved in prostitution. Actions that are funded include arts and outdoor pursuits, team working and confidence building as well as, for example, interview skills. It is designed to offer a bridge between a chaotic lifestyle and the labour market. Although projects have different objectives, many do not place a fixed time limit on the individual to gain these skills and begin to address their chaotic lifestyles. The New Futures Fund funded 103 projects with a total of £13.5 million (€22 million). Of 626 clients who moved on, 13% gained employment, 18% moved into further education, 9% into a government training programme, 6% into voluntary work and around 4% into pre-vocational training. Evaluation of the programme has proved positive and additional funding, for at least a further three years, has recently been agreed by government. However, the NFF approach remains a pilot scheme, which only exists in a few areas of Scotland. Following the positive evaluation it is disappointing that it has not been extended to the whole of Scotland, or indeed across the UK as a whole.

Integration of employment and resettlement

A second approach to facilitate access to employment for homeless people has been the integration of employment and resettlement initiatives. Examples of such initiatives are evident in many countries. The 'foyer' projects begun in France are well known and have spread to other countries with varied success. A common strategy is the establishment of businesses run and managed by homeless people. Examples are to be found in restaurants and office supply and graphic design services in Brussels, Vienna and Rotterdam. A good example is the Pension Maaszicht in Rotterdam, which is a halfway house that offers accommodation, work experience and training programmes and support to young homeless people. The young people prepared a business plan and secured investment from a bank to open a restaurant. Pension Maaszicht has been in operation for eight years and offers accommodation to 32 young people. The restaurant project provides a range of practical skills as well as teaching mutual cooperation and social skills, and is integral to successful resettlement.

In France the Fonds de Solidarite Logement (FSL) is used as a mechanism to facilitate access to housing for those in employment. In the framework of this fund, LOCA-PASS has been established. The aim of LOCA-PASS is to facilitate access to private or public rented accommodation for four social categories: employees of the private sector (regardless of their seniority and the nature of their contract), employees in the public sector, young people below 30 years (inter alia under professional training, being employed or looking for a job), and students. LOCA-PASS is therefore managed and funded by the public organisations which collect 1% solidarity contributions from employers. They work in partnership with the *Union économique et sociale du logement* (UESL) as well as with representatives of civil society. LOCA-PASS provides a guarantee and a monetary advance to future (young) tenants, which enable them to meet the conditions of the housing rental contract. The guarantee covers up to 18 months of rent including charges. The advance is granted at no cost and can either be paid to the tenant or the owner. The granting of the LOCA-PASS guarantee and/or advance is automatic when the applicant meets the conditions of the project. One extra condition concerns the monthly rent of the dwelling. A table of maximum rents is used, taking into account also regional price differentials across the country (ranging from 12.5 square metres in the Parisian area to 5.5 in most rural municipalities). Another condition concerns the income level of the applicants, making also a distinction between Ile-de-France and the rest of the country. The applicant submits a request to the public housing collection office that is nearest to her/his place of residence. If there is no reply within eight days, the assistance is considered granted. The UESL aimed to have at least 60,000 assists in 2000, while in reality more than 49,000 advances and nearly 29,000 guarantees were provided. Two thirds of these interventions have been directed to people younger than 30 years of age. A similar level of intervention had already been achieved in the first three months of 2001.

Preventing the risks of exclusion

Much has been written about the causes of homelessness, and there is general consensus on the multidimensional nature of the problem (Edgar et al, 2000). It is also understood that, in all EU member states, homelessness is an evolving phenomenon and the profile of the homeless population is constantly changing. It is at least arguable that the costs of preventing homelessness will be less than the social and economic costs of finding a solution after people have become homeless. Prevention of the risks of homelessness involves action on their underlying causes as well as intervention to deal with the triggers of homelessness. This involves both housing support (rent allowances, housing management action, housing advice) and social support (personal support and counselling; see Edgar et al [2000] for a discussion). In this section we consider three strategies to the prevention of the risks of housing exclusion: the implementation of local homelessness strategies, prevention of eviction, and action to enable vulnerable households to sustain a tenancy.

Implementation of homelessness strategies

The production of the first NAPs/incl in 2001 provided a policy framework in each European country within which interventions to deal with homelessness and the causes of homelessness could be assessed. The reduction in homelessness will be one of the indicators of success in achieving a socially inclusive society. The prevention and reduction of homelessness can neither be achieved by a single programme of action nor by monitoring the impact of the uncoordinated programmes of public and voluntary agencies. A number of countries have recognised the need for national homelessness strategies, the intention of which is to focus action in a planned and coordinated manner over a period of time to achieve defined targets. An important function of national strategies or programmes is to ensure that homelessness is adopted as a priority by a range of public agencies including those who, in the past, may not have been particularly preoccupied with homelessness.

Finland produced its first programme to reduce homelessness for the period 1987-1991. The aim was to abolish homelessness by 1991, both through general measures within housing policy as well as by special measures. This goal was included in the development plan for housing for the period. The national plan for social and health affairs also included the goal of providing an apartment for each homeless person in need of housing services as provided under the social care legislation. The level of homelessness was almost halved during the plan period. The second action programme has recently been approved and a working group has been established to monitor progress.

The Scottish Parliament has recently approved an action plan for the prevention of and effective response to homelessness (Scottish Executive, 2001). This plan focuses on four issues:

- improvements in homelessness legislation;
- housing supply, housing benefits and allowances;
- action to prevent homelessness;
- action to deliver an effective response to homelessness.

The improvement in homelessness legislation, brought about by the Housing Scotland Act 2001, places a duty on local authorities to draw up homelessness strategies. As we noted earlier, the Scottish Executive has issued guidance to local authorities requiring them to undertake a review of homelessness and to produce their strategies by April 2003 and has provided additional funding for this purpose. The Homelessness Act 2002 places a similar duty on English local authorities. The guidance to local authorities details the approach to be adopted in undertaking the homelessness review and the structure and purpose of the strategy. The homelessness review is required to assess the causes and scale of homelessness and to match this against the mapping of existing housing and support services in order to identify gaps in provision. Consultation with homeless people and a wide range of public and private sector agencies is recommended, and many authorities have created a local homelessness forum for this purpose. A strong emphasis is placed on prevention and joint working.

The Irish government's policy document, *Homelessness: An integrated strategy*, published in May 2000, sets out an inter-agency approach to tackling the problems of homelessness in a coordinated manner. The main elements of the strategy are:

- A homeless forum to be established in each county for the delivery of services to the homeless, made up of representatives from the local authorities, the health board and the relevant voluntary bodies operating in the county.
- Joint three-year action plans to be drawn up by local authorities and health boards, in cooperation with the voluntary bodies.
- More accommodation of a suitable type and of greater variety to be provided.
- Settlement and outreach programmes to be provided to assist homeless people to return to independent living.
- Capital spending by local authorities on accommodation for homeless persons over the five years 2001–5 to be doubled from €25.4 million to €50.8 million.
- Additional current funding of €7.6 million per annum to be available from 2001 from the Department of the Environment and Local Government to fund the provision of accommodation by local authorities and to establish settlement and outreach services.
- Additional current funding of €7.6 million a year to be available from 2001 from the Department of Health and Children to fund the provision of in-house care in accommodation for homeless persons.
- Each health board to carry out an assessment of the needs of homeless adults in its area.
- Preventative strategies are to be developed and implemented.

The strategy also clarifies the responsibilities of local authorities and of health boards. Local authorities have responsibility for the provision of accommodation for homeless adults as part of their overall housing responsibility and health boards are responsible for the health and care needs of homeless adults. Under the 1991 Childcare Act, health boards are responsible for meeting the accommodation and other needs of homeless children, that is, persons under the age of 18. The Department of the Environment and Local Government, through the local authorities, fund the non-care elements of the cost of providing accommodation for homeless adults as well as settlement and outreach staff. The Department of Health and Children, through the health boards, fund the care and welfare staff involved in providing in-house care, while at the same time meeting the health and welfare needs of homeless adults. The Youth Homelessness Strategy, launched in October 2001, complements the strategy on adult homelessness and provides a strategic framework within which youth homelessness is to be tackled on a national basis.

Prevention of eviction

Eviction from one's home can occur for a variety of reasons. Where a legal tenancy exists, eviction can occur at the termination of the lease period or where there has been a breach of the tenancy contract, often as a result of rent arrears or antisocial behaviour. Where a normal tenancy does not exist, then the reasons for eviction may be unrelated to the housing contract and the process of eviction may be more arbitrary and afford the household little protection under the law. Limited security of tenure exists in the informal housing market, but can also occur in the 'secondary housing market' (Sahlin, 2001) or in supported housing (Edgar and Mina-Coull, 1998). For a home owner, the loss of one's home can occur as a result of repossession by the lender for mortgage default. Whatever the reason for eviction, the loss of one's home is a traumatic event that normally, though not inevitably, leads to homelessness. It is often associated with a heightened risk of housing instability and repeated episodes of homelessness. Strategies to prevent housing eviction need to be different for each of these situations.

The increase in housing costs across all countries in Europe has been discussed in Chapters Three and Four of this volume. It is to be expected, in this context, that there is a greater risk of homelessness arising from housing payment problems. The dynamics underlying unsustainable housing commitments has been under-researched and are therefore not well understood (Burrows, 1998). We may assume, however, the importance of structural, financial and personal factors in determining housing payment problems (Boheim and Taylor, 2000). Therefore, rising housing costs are not the sole cause of the perceived increase in housing indebtedness. Whatever the causes involved, there is evidence of an increase in evictions arising from rent arrears. In the UK the increase of evictions demonstrates a marked variation between social landlords providing evidence of wide variation in housing management practices. In Germany, Busch-

Geertsema (2001) refers to the fact that one fifth of municipalities have some form of cooperation agreement which includes financial compensation for potential cases of rent arrears and of costs of eviction procedures for individual households ('individual guarantees'). The level of such guarantees is normally quite low (100-200 households in cities such as Bremen, Stuttgart and Duisburg). The city of Cologne is cited as an exception with nearly 11,000 declarations of surety for individuals (Busch-Geertsema, 2001, p 28). Busch-Geertsema reminds us that social landlords normally operate to performance standards that assume a loss of around 2% of the rent revenue due to bad debts and arrears. The prevention of eviction in these circumstances involves a balance of these standards coupled with allowance for enhanced housing management support to families to cope with their housing debt. The use of special guarantees for risky households (who otherwise may not be housed) can then be limited.

Eviction arising from antisocial behaviour is also an increasing problem. This may, in part, be a result of allocation policies aimed at maintaining a social balance in housing estates and hence a lower tolerance of noise or nuisance. In part it may reflect the fact that some households, young people in particular, require training to sustain a tenancy. Supported tenancies for young people aim to prevent antisocial behaviour by providing training. One innovative project started in Dundee (Scotland) in 1996 combines supported housing, dispersed tenancies and outreach prevention work to provide a service for antisocial families. The nature of antisocial behaviour varied (neighbour conflict, property damage, mental health problems, child-control problems). An evaluation study demonstrated that the project stabilised families' housing situation, avoiding costs associated with eviction, homelessness administration and rehousing (Dillane et al, 2001).

Sahlin (2001) raises two distinct issues regarding eviction from housing in Sweden in the context of the right of access to housing. First, she quotes Hemstrom (2000) who argues that the Swedish housing market, which was never strongly regulated, was governed through the use of government subsidies, the withdrawal of which has left the market exposed. There is therefore a need for procedures to regulate eviction. Second, Sahlin refers to the dilemma facing vulnerable households in the 'secondary housing market'. Tenants requiring support, including homeless people, are normally subtenants of the support provider and have no direct enforceable rights to prevent eviction if the supervision or support arrangements fail. Attempts to introduce greater legislative protection from eviction for people on 'special contracts' have been resisted on the grounds that an increased tenure security for people in special housing would render the housing market even less flexible.

There is evidence, in some countries, of home owners losing their homes as a result of mortgage repossession. In Britain between 1990 and 1996 over one million individuals were subject to mortgage repossession (Council of Mortgage Lenders, 1997, quoted in Ford and Burrows, 1999). There are some limited examples of building societies cooperating with housing associations to purchase the dwelling and provide the delinquent owner with a tenancy.

The importance of information and advice in preventing eviction and homelessness is well recognised. In Scotland, local authorities are required under recent legislation to ensure that advice about housing and other related services is available free of charge to any persons who consider themselves to be at risk from homelessness. As an example of a local initiative, the Scottish Council for Single Homelessness has produced an educational pack aimed at school children, which is in use in many secondary schools in Scotland. In England, Shelter has recently launched a toll-free telephone helpline. An emergency telephone number in France (115) provides a similar service.

Maintaining tenancies in the rental housing market

Strategies to remove or reduce the financial barriers of access to the housing market have developed, especially, in countries with a large private rented housing sector and limited access to social housing. Examples of the emergence of 'social rental agencies' (SRAs) can be found in both northern and southern European countries including Belgium, Germany, Italy and Spain. Although their structure and operation differs, their underlying objective remains the same, removing financial barriers and enabling vulnerable tenants to sustain a tenancy by guaranteeing the risks to the private landlord.

De Decker (2001, 2002) describes the genesis of SRAs in Belgium. Social rental agencies are part of an approach to ensure adequate and affordable housing provision for vulnerable households by socialising the private rental market. This effectively means the withdrawal of the management of private rental accommodation from the mechanisms of the market and its replacement by 'social management'. The objectives of the SRAs are rent mediation on the private rental market, linkage of housing and welfare work, and the development of local policy networks on affordable housing. Legal recognition of the SRAs by all three regional governments in Belgium has aimed to increase the number of dwellings available to vulnerable households. This is achieved by linking housing provision with guidance and support for tenants and by guaranteeing socially adjusted rents. The approach of the SRAs should also improve the quality of the accommodation offered to vulnerable households.

The primary activity of social rental agencies is the (sub)letting of housing units to vulnerable households. Social rental agencies obtain dwellings by either renting on both the private and the public rental markets or by purchasing housing outright. The tenants of SRAs are former clients of social welfare institutions who are at risk of homelessness, re-institutionalisation or unregulated private renting. For these vulnerable households, SRAs provide affordable housing along with housing security according to federal tenancy laws. The benefits to the tenant are manifest in the provision of accommodation at reasonable rents, long leases and the possibility of support provided by the nominating agency. Agreements on rent deposits and furniture form part of an overall package as do contractual arrangements for the provision of support by partner agencies where required.

The social management component of the SRA is characterised by its cooperative, but nevertheless firm, attitude towards the tenant and the feedback it provides to the nominating institution. Support to the tenant remains the responsibility of the nominating institution or service. In the event of a breach of contract or the manifestation of challenging behaviour, the SRA is responsible for alerting the nominating agency that is, in turn, responsible for organising and delivering an appropriate programme of support to remedy the situation. As part of their overall aim to minimise the risks of homelessness, re-institutionalisation and/or unregulated renting, SRAs have developed strategies to help tenants manage any rent arrears. These include individualised housing management support packages that are delivered either by the nominating institution, the SRA itself or a combination of both. When tenants do develop rent arrears, SRAs seldom opt for eviction. Instead, they seek to identify the reasons for non-payment in order to arrange appropriate support. If, in the long term and despite support from the placement agency, rent arrears persist, re-institutionalisation may be considered. It could therefore be argued that SRAs aim to prevent homelessness due to eviction through an individualised package of appropriate housing and support as necessary.

The considerable increase in the number of SRAs and the growth in the size of their stock may be attributed to the wider acceptance of the concept of housing with support in light of the shift from institutional living to community-based living arrangements for vulnerable people. By October 1997, there were 64 SRAs in Flanders and 18 in Wallonia. The development of SRAs in the Brussels-Capital Region was slower and may be explained by the complex institutional context and a lack of money.

In Italy, 'social real property' activities follow two basic methods of operation. First, they make the private rental market accessible. This uses similar methods to the Belgian SRAs, mobilising the supply of accommodation and offering intermediation services, guarantees to owners and supplementary financial assistance. The focus is on disadvantaged groups and specifically on immigrants. Second, the agencies set up and manage a stock of rented accommodation (as permanent or temporary accommodation, long or medium term) at low prices drawing on public (public sector stock and funds) and private/associations 'solidarity' resources. The promoters of these initiatives are mostly associations, cooperatives and private welfare operators with partnership relations with the public sector. This activity is, however, only significant in a few regions of the centre and north of the country. Similarly, the Pro-Housing association in Spain has, since 1997, operated a programme of support for "the integration through housing of collectives with difficulties" (Carbrera, 2001, p 41). This programme aims to mediate between the private housing market and people who have difficulties accessing housing including people with mental health problems, ex-offenders, drug addicts, immigrants, single parent families at risk of eviction and vulnerable young people. The programme operates through the use of rent guarantees and support for tenants.

Similar agencies (*Soziale Wohnraumhilfen*) have existed in Germany since the late 1980s. These are described in detail elsewhere (see Edgar et al, 1999; Busch-Geertsema, 2001). Perhaps a distinctive feature of the German housing assistance agencies is the fact that they target specific groups (single homeless, ex-convicts, physically abused women, vulnerable young people and people with mental health problems). In addition to the emergence of specific social rental agencies, the German experience has built on the use of contractual agreements between the municipalities and private landlords or housing companies. This approach is significant in the context of the increasing 'marketisation' of social housing agencies described in earlier chapters of this volume.

The 'protected market segment' (*geschütztes Marktsegment*) in Berlin and the 'contract for the improvement of housing provision for households with a certificate of being in urgent need of housing' (*Wohnungsnotstandsvertrag*) in Bremen are well documented examples of this approach (Busch-Geertsema, 2001). In Berlin a special agreement was reached in November 1993 to introduce a protected market segment for people who are homeless or threatened by homelessness. A contract was signed between the municipality and those 19 housing companies in Berlin in which the municipality holds ownership shares of more than 51%. The 'municipal' housing companies committed themselves to provide a fixed number of 2,000 dwellings per annum of the fluctuation in their housing stock for the provision of the target group. The target groups focussed on people threatened by eviction and homeless persons who have been living for at least one year in Berlin, who do not have a tenancy of their own, and who cannot procure normal housing by their own efforts. To compensate housing providers for economic risks a municipal guarantee was given for financial losses connected with tenancies in the protected market segment during the first three years of each tenancy. In six years, nearly 8,000 households got a permanent tenancy under this contract. Although problems were registered for nearly 30% of the tenancies, the number of tenancies ending in an eviction was only about 1.8% of all market segment tenancies. In the year 2000, new financial and organisational agreements with service agencies in the voluntary sector were reached including services 'to achieve and sustain tenancies' and explicitly mentioning social support for tenants of the protected market segment as one of the relevant tasks under this heading. This initiative, although successful, remains unique in Germany.

Helping the most vulnerable

A clear association has been identified between de-institutionalisation and homelessness and housing exclusion. De-institutionalisation is associated with the closure of long-stay psychiatric hospitals and the development of care in the community. However, all people who experience a period of institutional living may require assistance to gain access to the housing market. This can also include young people leaving care, ex-offenders and men leaving the armed forces. Different approaches to helping the most vulnerable gain access to housing can be described. The development of support in housing is important both in the prevention of homelessness and in the resettlement of homeless people (Edgar et al, 2000). In some countries legislation makes specific provision or funding available for identified vulnerable groups. In addition, non-governmental organisations (NGOs) focus services on specific groups. The spatial concentration of the most vulnerable is reflected in area-based strategies to deal with poor housing and urban regeneration.

Support and housing

The provision of support and housing has been identified as a key strategy in tackling housing exclusion and in the prevention of homelessness for the most vulnerable. The strategies for meeting the support needs of vulnerable groups to enable them to access housing or to sustain a tenancy are diverse.

The UK has perhaps gone furthest in developing this strategy in Europe. At a macro level there has been a strong emphasis in the UK on what the government has termed 'joined-up thinking' which has placed a new emphasis on cross-departmental cooperation within the statutory sector. At national level there is a new requirement to draw up housing support strategies in preparation for a new funding mechanism (called Supporting People) to be introduced in 2003. This involves mapping all housing support services in each local authority area and assessing unmet needs. The requirement is for a coordinating group to be formed incorporating all relevant stakeholders, including voluntary sector and statutory providers.

A recent paper by the national coalition service providers for the homeless in Germany (*Bundesarbeitsgemeinschaft Wohnungslosenhilfe, BAGW* – see BAGW, 2000) emphasises that while, on the one hand, every citizen should have a right to normal housing as long as he or she wishes, but that, on the other hand, cooperation between social work and housing providers is essential to enable access to housing for those people who are particularly difficult to integrate. Financial risks should be covered by special guarantees and also by transferring a proportion of social security payments directly to landlords to ensure regular rent payment. The paper also calls for a better coordination in the allocation of housing and support for households that are difficult to integrate (for example, by an independent clearing agency) and for a better use of instruments such as case management and conferences (BAGW, 2000, p 160).

Specific vulnerable groups

We discussed in earlier chapters groups who are specifically referred to in legislation as eligible for support or protection as a result of their vulnerability in the housing market. While the identity of these groups varied across the member states, they include: vulnerable young people, women fleeing domestic violence, single parents, people with a mental health problem, people with a learning disability, people with physical disabilities, people leaving institutional care, and vulnerable older people. In some countries specific groups are identified as requiring assistance. These include, for example, travellers in Ireland, Greek repatriates from Pontos, gypsies in Spain and Greece, 'unusual characters' in Denmark. In almost all countries, two specific groups are considered to be more at risk of housing exclusion than other groups: immigrants/asylum seekers and young people.

To address the needs of marginalised and homeless people, the Ministry of Housing and Urban Affairs in Denmark introduced the Unusual Dwellings to Unusual Characters initiative in 1998 (see also Chapter Five of this volume). The initiative was planned to run over a four-year period and a fund was set up where local innovators could apply for funding. From January 2001 the initiative has been made permanent and integrated in the Social Housing Act (§146a). In December 2000, 15 projects were funded with 115 dwellings. Three of the projects are located in the Municipality of Copenhagen, one of which – the Illu-Housing Project for Greenlanders – is highly innovative. Research showed that homeless Greenlanders would like to be close to the sea and that they like to sleep in the open. The plan is to locate the Illu-housing in the southern harbour of Copenhagen and to involve Greenlanders in the construction of their houses. The plan is that ordinary installations, the toilet and kitchen, are constructed by formal artisans, while Greenlanders construct the rest of the house themselves with the municipality paying for the materials. One of the many positive aspects of the initiative is that the cost of construction is generally low (Nordgaard and Koch-Nielsen, 2001).

In the Netherlands, a review of the policy support needed to enable municipalities to undertake an enabling and coordinating role on the issue of homeless young people was conducted in 2001. The aim was to sign a national covenant on homeless young people with national stakeholders in 2002. The assistance to homeless young people will be supported in part by additional funding (€50 million) made available to improve coordination between local youth policy and youth welfare.

The social housing sector in Austria does not make provision for the needs of young adults who therefore have to compete on the private housing market for the relatively small number of affordable housing units. Following empirical research in a number of counties, which established the scale of the problem of homelessness among young people, an emergency shelter was established in Salzburg. Under the title Exit 7, this shelter had contact with over 100 young people during its first year of operation, about half of whom were young women. The funding contract established between Exit 7 and the county's youth welfare office restricts the upper age limit for clients to 19 years. There is concern that the youth welfare office will restrict this further to 16 years. The existing provisions by homeless services are not adequate to meet the specific needs of vulnerable young people aged 16-21. The lack of provision for the housing needs of this age group leads inevitably to hidden homelessness and increased vulnerability.

In contrast to the lack of provision in Austria, voluntary organisations have been established in a number of countries to work specifically with vulnerable young people. In Greece, the Arsis agency works exclusively with socially excluded young people and young offenders. The work of Arsis has focussed particularly on homelessness as it affects this target group, emphasising especially the problems faced by young people leaving care or reform institutions. However, the provision of temporary accommodation and support services has been affected by a lack of funding and a reliance on charitable donations.

Action in areas marked by exclusion

In Portugal, one of the most disadvantaged groups who lacked access to decent and sanitary housing was to be found among the shanty-town dwellers. *Programmea Especial de Realojamento* (PER, or Special Reallocation Programme) was established by law in mid-1993 with the aim to eradicate the shanty towns by 2001. The greatest impact of PER was in the metropolitan areas of Lisbon and Porto, each of which comprises a main municipality (Lisbon and Porto, respectively) and a set of neighbouring municipalities. These are the areas where the phenomenon of the 'barracks' and shanty towns mainly occur. It is estimated that the programme benefited around 70,000 families (Machado, 1997, p 11) the majority of whom lived in Lisbon (35,000) or Porto (15,000).

A study commissioned by the National Institute of Housing argued that the PER should be used as a strategic programme against discrimination and social exclusion (rather than be a programme for strengthening the social ghettos that many of the existing social quarters represent; Vieira et al, 1993). This aim implied the need to integrate the rehousing programmes into programmes of community social development that may include, simultaneously, problems related with employment, education, occupational training and health. This proved a major undertaking since the survey and inventory of the barracks and families estimated that 48,558 flats were needed to replace 42,000 barracks. The legislation that established PER had some innovative features for Portugal at the time, including new funding mechanisms and the development of public sector and voluntary sector partnership. The development of the rehousing programme within the wider social inclusion programme was innovative in itself. Other innovatory aspects of the programme were the possibility for families to develop their own solutions for their housing problems, and the establishment of specific solutions for groups with particular characteristics.

Teixeira et al (1997) discuss the impact of the PER programme in relation to the governance of housing, the development of integrated approaches to housing and urban regeneration and, for some municipalities, the integration of housing and social inclusion programmes. One of the issues that gained new relevance and debate concerned the roles of the central government and the local authorities in the field of housing. The PER was the initiative of central government who invested heavily in the programme. On the other hand, the municipalities have the responsibility of ensuring the maintenance of the houses built under this programme, as well as the aspects related with the social groups covered. It is also the responsibility of the municipalities to provide land for the new buildings and pay the debt service of the loans (Morais, 1997). Most of the local authorities involved adopted a multidimensional approach to the problem. As a result, the programme led to the involvement of various municipal services (planning, projects and works, urban management, financial administration, housing, culture, education and social action). This did not always result in the integration of action into a comprehensive and coherent strategy. However, it did encourage greater coordination. Half of the municipalities involved developed the programme within the objective of social insertion of the population (Texeira et al, 1997). Some municipalities – namely, Lisbon – adopted a strategy that consisted of decentralising the implementation of PER to NGOs that expressed a willingness to take charge of the process in a certain area. This strategy shortened the period of implementation, allowed greater proximity to the population and fostered the consideration of the other social aspects of the problem.

Mobilising all relevant actors

The development of multi-agency approaches in decision making and service delivery in relation to homelessness have become increasingly common in recent years. This is perceived to be necessary in part due to the often complex and interrelated needs of homeless people. Multi-agency approaches are promoted as good practice both in the prevention and in the alleviation of homelessness. However, the call for integration of action is more common at the strategic and planning levels than at the operational levels of action (see Edgar et al, 1999).

Within the context of the EU programme to combat poverty and social exclusion, mobilising all relevant actors can be understood to have several distinct aspects of action. First, it involves horizontal integration of policies – joined-up thinking – among all levels of government agencies. This implies a 'mainstreaming' of homelessness as a policy priority across all government agencies. Second, it involves partnership action to address the needs of particular vulnerable groups (for example, caravan dwellers, travellers, gypsies) or disadvantaged areas (such as shanty towns). Third, it involves multi-agency working to improve the provision of services for homeless people and to meet the demands of individualised care/resettlement plans. Multi-agency working is also increasingly necessary as a result of the changes in governance occurring in the last decade, reflected particularly in the changing role of public agencies (local authorities and health boards) from providers of services to purchasers and commissioners.

Coordination of action

Under the 2002 Homelessness Act in England, local authorities will be obliged to work with all relevant stakeholders to draw up strategies to prevent and alleviate homelessness. This is already a requirement under the Scottish Housing Act 2001. Linked with this is a new requirement in Scotland for health authorities to assess the health needs of homelessness in their area of operation and ensure that those needs are addressed. A new post of Health and Homelessness Coordinator has been established in the Scottish Executive to oversee this aspect of joined-up thinking. Similar approaches have been described earlier in this chapter in relation to homelessness strategies being developed in Ireland and in Finland.

As a response to the multivariate problems in Danish social housing estates during the early 1990s, the Urban Committee was established in 1993. It has been described as the biggest urban effort in Denmark in the 1990s. This initiative has a collective approach, addressing the exclusion of whole housing areas, and trying to integrate and thereby improve the quality of life for all the residents on a housing estate. In this way, the initiative breaks with previous tendencies in social policy that aimed at more individualistic approaches. Six ministries are involved in the initiative with the Ministry of Social Affairs and the Ministry of Housing and Urban Affairs providing leadership and coordination. The latter has chairmanship for the initiative. The Urban Committee has succeeded in improving the quality of life of the tenants already living in the areas, by solving many of the social problems existing on the estates. Tenant advisers on estates help prevent a process of social exclusion of the vulnerable tenants. An evaluation of the initiative showed, that the tenant advisers have not been good at keeping in contact with the most socially excluded people (Skifter Andersen, 1999). Changes have been established to improve this in the future. The Urban Committee also succeeded in lowering rent by rearranging loans. This was accompanied by a decrease in mobility on estates by 13% between 1994 and 1997 (Skifter Andersen, 1999, p 12). The mobility decrease should, however, be viewed in the light of the general tendency to a housing shortage in Denmark and the increase in prices on ownership dwellings, which might have contributed to the decrease.

Local partnerships

In Spain, local partnerships have emerged to deal with the problems faced by shanty-town dwellers in gaining access to decent housing. Boadilla del Monte is a village of 20,000 inhabitants, located 14 kilometres from Madrid. In 1997, about 300 people were living in shanty dwellings made from waste materials of metal and wood. The shanty dwellers were all adult men from Morocco with an average age of 35. Most of them had an income from temporary and sporadic jobs in construction or gardening. The council asked the Pro-Housing Association to coordinate a programme integrating housing, employment, social support and education. This involved a number of public and voluntary agencies including:

- Boadilla del Monte Town Council: coordinating the participating organisations and guaranteeing the financial support of the project;
- *La Encina*, the inter-municipal association: in charge of coordinating the education and employment programmes, the minors' programme and the minimum wage programme;
- the Red Cross and Doctors of the World: giving health care to those who could not use the general health services;
- the Diocesan Delegation of Emigration from *Getafe* and ASTI: taking care of social support for the beneficiaries of the programme and helping in literacy and adult education and legal advice;
- the Pro-Housing Association: responsible for housing and support.

The programme has made progress in eliminating the shanty-town settlements and rehousing 220 people.

A second example is the shanty town of Peñagrande located in the north of Madrid. Gypsy families living in shanty dwellings started to rent their shacks to North African immigrants. In May 1993 there were 207 shanty dwellings and 675 inhabitants. A fire in October 1994, which left 60 families roofless, made the accommodation situation urgent. A development programme was initiated involving a local partnership of agencies including:

- the Ministry of Labour and Social Services;
- the Health and Social Services of the Madrid Region;
- Madrid Town Council;
- the Municipal Board of Fuencarral-El Pardo;
- the Pro-Housing Association;
- the Centre of Social Action of San Rafael;
- the Association of Moroccan Immigrant Workers (ATIME).

The social services of the Municipal Board of Fuencarral-El Pardo, with the Centre of Social Action of San Rafael, deal with applications for accommodation and provide grants to pay rent for a maximum period of two years during which time the grants decrease progressively until they disappear. The Pro-Housing Association selects accommodation from the rented housing market appropriate to the families' needs. The association signs a rental contract with the owner and cedes the use of the accommodation to the family in writing. The programme assures owners the payment of the rent and protects the house with a multiple risk policy for the first two years. During this period the Pro-Housing Association provides social support to tenants. It serves as mediator between the owners and the tenants or between the tenants and the neighbours in case of dispute. The Ministry of Labour and Social Affairs, the Town Council and the Madrid Regional Government all supply important economic and material resources. A total of 614 people from the shanty town have been rehoused by these means.

Multi-agency working

The established literature on the benefits of and barriers to effective multi-agency working is too extensive to review here (see Kennedy et al [2001] for a discussion of the UK experience). We have commented elsewhere (Edgar et al, 1999) that time-limited funding of initiatives, competition for limited resources among diverse voluntary sector agencies and public sector commissioning arrangements can all stifle good practice in inter-agency working.

The project at La Roche sur Yon (Vendée) in France began in 1995 with, as a key objective, the organisation and networking of existing services in the area to provide service users with a diverse yet integrated series of options to meet their various and complex needs. Focusing on the empowerment of the service users, the project not only explicitly involves users in decision making with regard to the choice of services appropriate to their needs, but also involves them as active partners in specific elements of the work. A wide range of agencies, both statutory and voluntary, are involved in the project. It operates as a loosely constructed partnership with the Direction Départementale de l'Action Sanitaire et Sociale (DDASS) taking the lead in the creation of the project and the coordination of the day reception centre. The mobilisation of statutory agencies such as the DDASS, the Caisse d'Allocations Familiales (CAF) and the Centre Communal d'Action Sociale (CCAS), is of particular interest since it signals a departure from the norm in France where statutory agencies are seldom inclined to work in true partnership with voluntary sector agencies or with housing associations. In this instance, a broader interpretation of legislative frameworks for the delivery of services has enabled statutory agencies to become real partners.

In Luxembourg, *Wunnenngshellef* was commissioned by the Ministry of the Family in order to act as a central housing negotiation service enabling member associations, who provide short-term accommodation and/or support services, to move clients on to more long-term accommodation with continuing support. Since *Wunnengshellef* is responsible for identifying, preparing and managing housing while the member agencies are responsible for support services and referrals, a wider range of client groups with diverse needs can have access to housing in a more cost effective way. By working cooperatively, each member agency can both contribute its expertise and share a common understanding of the multidimensional characteristics of homelessness. The involvement of private and public sector landlords in the project also helps to raise their awareness of issues of homelessness while maximising the use of existing resources.

The San Marcellino project in Italy involves coordination with public and voluntary sector agencies and the development of flexible and long-term solutions based on individual care plans. In an attempt to provide an integrated service, San Marcellino cooperates with a range of agencies including:

- Caritas (Centro Monastero) which operates a similar service;
- the Local Authority (night) Shelter (referrals);
- CAD (public sector social services for the elderly/rent subsidy);
- mental health services (joint case work plans);
- the Local Authority Solidarity Office (finance).

A Technical Operational Group, consisting of representatives from the district social services offices, the municipal shelter, San Marcellino, and Caritas, has been established with the aim of defining responsibilities and finding common methods of working. Therefore, the project may best be described as adopting a network approach rather than a partnership approach.

In their review of the literature in the UK, Kennedy et al (2001) refer to three examples of existing practice in multi-agency working on homelessness in order to illustrate different problems and issues involved. The first example they cite in order to demonstrate that multi-agency working needs to develop organically and cannot be imposed from above. This example is The Hub housing advice centre in Bristol which incorporates staff from voluntary, statutory and national organisations working together to meet the needs of single homeless people. They also suggest that the prior existence of networks between the agencies was necessary to facilitate the process. The second example is used to demonstrate the need for a 'one-stop shop' provision to reach the most vulnerable street homeless who may be excluded from mainstream services and for generic workers, linked to 'multi-agency panels', to deal with the complex problems presented by the most vulnerable. This is the Under One Roof project in London, which is a partnership of 30 statutory and voluntary organisations seeking to address the needs of vulnerable rough sleepers. The final example, of a supported housing project, is cited to demonstrate the fact that, even where inter-agency working is well planned, collaboration is often poor at the points where people access services when the opportunity to look holistically at clients' needs is missed.

Conclusion

Intervention strategies to tackle homelessness have changed in recent years from a focus on control and emergency intervention to strategies aimed at prevention and resettlement. This shift in focus represents a change in perspective towards a 'social model' of homelessness and has been associated with innovation in both public policy response and service provision. However, it is only with the adoption of the European social agenda to combat poverty and social exclusion that a European policy dimension has emerged. In this chapter we have attempted to consider how existing strategies of intervention and examples of service provision fit within the policy objectives agreed at Nice in December 2000.

The European programme to combat poverty and social exclusion rightly identifies the multidimensional nature of homelessness and hence stresses the need for more 'joined-up policies'. The review presented here confirms that there remains a distinct geography of homelessness, and that differential access to decent and affordable housing is evident in all countries. Therefore, national strategies to deal with homelessness and housing exclusion must clearly be combined with local strategies reflecting the needs of particular housing markets and the nature of vulnerability they create.

Some countries have specific laws formulated around the concept of the right to housing (see also Chapter Two of this volume). While this does not guarantee housing for homeless people and other vulnerable groups, it is arguable that some statutory framework is a necessary adjunct to an inclusive housing strategy. In a comparable situation, the disability rights lobby has been a powerful force in empowering a formerly marginalised (and often institutionalised) group of people and in bending mainstream policies and programmes to meet their needs. There is evidence that recent legislation, especially in the northern European countries (the UK, Ireland, Germany, Sweden and Finland for example), has defined groups at risk in the housing market and has tended to widen priority categories in a more inclusive manner than hitherto. Despite this, the needs of the homeless tend not to be dealt with in a coherent manner in the first round of NAPs/incl, and it remains the case that the allocation of social housing is still often left to local discretion albeit within the framework of national guidance.

There is evidence that in areas where the housing market is overheated, such as Finland and Ireland, strategies have recently been adopted to increase the supply of housing for vulnerable groups and this has been evoked in the context of the adoption of a national homelessness strategy. Portugal is the only other country to adopt a strategy of (social) housing provision to meet the particular needs of shanty-town dwellers in the metropolitan areas.

Labour market exclusion and poverty are recognised as key factors associated with homelessness and the consumption of poor quality housing. Equally pathway models of understanding routes *into* homelessness suggest that strategies to provide sustainable routes *out* of homelessness need an integrated approach, incorporating employment, housing and social support. The objective to facilitate participation in employment as a key objective in developing social inclusion strategies is therefore to be welcomed. France would appear to be the only country to have a specific policy linking employment contributions and housing for defined categories of workers. The provision of basic educational and literacy skills for the most marginalised has been recognised. There are numerous examples of specific projects aimed to link employment and resettlement often targeted at particular groups such as the young. However, there appear to be few examples of employment initiatives targeted at the specific employment needs of homeless women.

The prevention of homelessness in the context of this debate on access to housing must clearly focus on the risks associated with the loss of a home and the support required to enable the most vulnerable to sustain a tenancy. Strategies to provide landlords with guarantees in relation to rental payments and housing management are manifest in many countries and take different forms – from a basic rent deposit scheme at one end of the spectrum to social rental agencies at the other. These approaches are evident in countries where rental housing is predominantly privately owned but are equally, and increasingly, applicable to social landlords.

Perhaps some of the most vulnerable groups in our society are those without the protection of citizenship. (A forthcoming book in this series will consider the particular problems of immigrants in the housing market.) A second group of vulnerable people are those who are at a high risk of institutional living if they can not access the support required to live independently in the community. These include young people leaving care, ex-offenders, those leaving the armed forces, and those with learning disabilities and mental health problems. The development of support in housing has attempted to meet these needs in many countries (see Edgar et al, 2000). The third group of households at risk includes those that are at a difficult transition stage in their life courses and who lack the family support or income to manage the transition effectively. This may include young people (entering the labour market), women fleeing physical and mental abuse, partners in a relationship breakdown and people retiring from the labour force. Some of these groups are specifically mentioned in legislation and others are assisted in social protection systems. A fourth group of people live in areas marked by social exclusion, and here policies of urban or housing regeneration have provided the main vehicle for assistance. Beyond these groups there are people with unusual lifestyles who may be difficult to include in mainstream housing or in traditional service provision. The needs of travellers are recognised in Ireland, the unusual housing needs of unusual characters are recognised in Denmark.

The success of these social inclusion objectives will depend on effective multi-agency working, improved coordination and partnership at the local level. This, just as much as the release of adequate financing of prevention and inclusion strategies, will be the main challenge for public sector and voluntary agencies alike.

SEVEN

Conclusions

The changing policy context

The EU programme to combat poverty and social exclusion represents an important shift in the policy debate in relation to homelessness. First, it places the debate on homelessness policy squarely within the discourse of poverty and social exclusion. Second, it introduces into the policy framework the need for governments to facilitate access to housing – even if this falls short of guaranteeing housing as a basic human right. Third, it recognises that the nature of homelessness is much broader than rooflessness or rough sleeping, and embraces forms of housing exclusion arising from houselessness, insecure housing and inadequate housing.

It is also apparent that the innovation in service provision for homeless people in recent years has, at the scale of delivery, been characterised by a shift from a reactive stance (aiming to alleviate the crisis by emergency provision), towards a proactive stance (aiming to prevent homelessness) (Edgar et al, 1999). This has been associated with a shift in policy perception of homelessness which recognises the structural and institutional causes of homelessness, rather than emphasising individual pathological explanations; a shift from a medical model to a social model.

In the context of a social inclusion agenda at national and EU level, this chapter examines the broad approaches of state intervention within the understanding developed in previous chapters in relation to the three spheres of integration. The first section of the chapter considers the meaning of prevention of housing exclusion and the policy implications of this objective. In the face of a persistence of homelessness in all its forms in Europe, the second section of the chapter considers why policy has had such limited impact in the past. This identifies common aspects of policy failure across Europe and highlights particular areas of concern. The third section attempts to draw on the lessons and experiences described in earlier chapters to distinguish the key elements of good practice, what is required to plan for good practice and what challenges face government and service providers in implementing good practice.

Social inclusion and the prevention of homelessness

A key organising framework of this book has been the consideration of the roles of the market, the state and civil society in facilitating access to housing and in understanding the factors that create vulnerability and risk of exclusion from the housing market. In the absence of a guaranteed right to housing, the commodification of housing has led to a growing exclusion of the most vulnerable and marginalised groups from access to decent and affordable housing. The agencies of civil society (the church and voluntary organisations) have been unable to significantly influence or moderate the structural factors that create homelessness, while individual coping strategies rely on informal markets and reciprocal relationships which can be exploitative as well as inclusionary. This points to the central importance of the role of state redistribution in facilitating access to affordable housing for low-income and vulnerable groups. However, following the retrenchment and 'hollowing out' of state activities in recent years, the redistributive role of the state across most EU countries has been severely curtailed. European political concern with issues of social exclusion and cohesion reflects the nature of the problems which have arisen as a consequence of the inadequacies and the combined failings of the market, civil society and the state in addressing such issues as access to adequate housing for the most vulnerable in society. In this context, the European programme to combat poverty and social exclusion potentially provides a framework for national action in that it embodies an important shift in policy focus by placing homelessness within the context of the debate on poverty and by focussing policy action on underlying structural factors.

Facilitating access to decent and affordable housing and the prevention of life crises such as homelessness are explicitly identified as among the key objectives of the European policy to combat poverty and social exclusion. The achievement of these objectives will require a combination of both direct and indirect intervention by the state. First, a rights-based approach that underpins a citizen's right to housing would allow for governments to be made accountable for ensuring this basic human right (see Sahlin, 2001). The right to housing is an essential requirement in facilitating access to housing for vulnerable groups. The statutory guarantee of access to housing can only be realised by the direct provision of an adequate supply of affordable good quality housing. This presupposes that effective methods of allocation and targeting are in place. This requires public control over the production of housing and its forms of tenure as well as over the allocation of dwellings to the most vulnerable – a protected market segment. Therefore, the right to housing needs to be operated through appropriate legal provisions to meet the needs of the homeless and vulnerable households for adequate and affordable housing and to provide security against arbitrary eviction. However, such an approach would exclude non-citizens of the EU and would therefore create political issues in devising strategies for the integration and assimilation of immigrants into European societies. (This important topic will be the subject of a future volume in this series.)

Second, strategies that combat poverty have the potential to provide key protection against housing exclusion. The adoption of inclusive social protection systems would guarantee that everyone has the income required to afford a decent minimum standard of housing. This may be achieved by different means appropriate to different welfare structures and include combinations of income support and housing subsidy and housing allowance. However, in order to be effective, such a system would need to be universally applied. This would require, for instance, the explicit inclusion of some of the most vulnerable groups such as single adults, who are often excluded from current social protection provision. Undoubtedly, this would give rise to political objection and might be difficult to realise. Furthermore, it would be difficult to develop consensus on what is meant by 'adequate housing' for all social groups; what would be the standards of adequacy for young people, for older people, for families and how would these vary across national contexts?

Even if access to housing is guaranteed by statutory provision and facilitated by adequate and universal income support, access to affordable housing for the homeless, for those vulnerable to housing exclusion, and for those experiencing a life crisis may only be realised by the provision of appropriate social support tailored to individual needs. This will be necessary, for example, for those who require support in order to live independently in the community, for those whose housing vulnerability has arisen as a result of interpersonal relationship breakdown, and for those (such as young people) who require support for a transitional period in their life course.

Whichever approach is considered, it is clear that particular groups (for example, immigrants, vulnerable single adults, and young people) may not be adequately protected from the risks of housing exclusion. Nevertheless, we would argue that a rights-based approach is the core foundation on which social protection systems, housing systems and social support can be brought to bear, to guarantee and facilitate access to housing for all citizens. Once the foundation of the right to a secure tenancy and affordable and decent housing is provided the means of implementing this will vary depending on the existing housing tenure systems and social protection systems.

Strategies of intervention will involve action aimed at prevention, alleviation and resettlement. While the nature of alleviation and resettlement approaches are reasonably well understood, the nature and principles underlying prevention strategies are perhaps less clear-cut. This is especially the case since the nature of vulnerability to housing exclusion will be different in different social welfare systems, will change over time in response to the dynamics of interaction between the three spheres of integration and will vary over the life course of the individual. Preventative action is required to address the causes of housing exclusion and homelessness at all levels – the structural, institutional, interpersonal and individual. At the structural level policies which are consistent with the principles of social justice and directly address poverty and housing supply will, of course, be necessary foundations for effective action to prevent homelessness. Homelessness strategies that integrate policies in employment, social services, health and related areas will also be important in providing a framework for prevention for different vulnerable groups (for example, young people, unemployed, homeless women, and those facing eviction). At the institutional level, the most basic method of prevention requires policies to ensure that people leaving institutional living situations of all forms (prison, psychiatric hospitals, care homes and the armed forces) have access to appropriate housing.

The principles of prevention at the level of interpersonal relationship and individual action are the most difficult to articulate. We have argued that access to housing is part of the 'capability set' that every individual requires to permit attainment of their universal rights and to shape their own life in cooperation and reciprocity with others (see discussion in Chapter Two of this volume; Sen, 1992; Nussbaum, 2000). The prevention of homelessness must therefore develop the capacities of individuals to enable them to exercise their rights. We suggest that this involves three areas of action involving support to:

- enable the exercise of choice;
- sustain personal relationships and social networks;
- facilitate independent living.

The most basic requirement to ensure access to housing, for any individual or household whatever their circumstances, is the ability to exercise choice in the housing market. To exercise choice the individual requires:

- adequate resources (the ability to pay);
- information (knowledge of alternative options);
- competence to contract (equality of status with other actors in the marketplace);
- and legal protection (from exploitation or fraud).

Adequate income, information and advice, freedom from discrimination and legal rights are all components of any strategy to improve the ability of individual households to sustain a tenancy.

The capacity of the individual household to cope is strengthened by strong reciprocal social networks and personal relationships. Homelessness is often caused by relationship breakdown and the route to reintegration involves rebuilding relationships or social networks or providing the competence to maintain an independent, autonomous household. Strategies of neighbourhood renewal, mediation services and family services, as well as support to individual homeless households, all have a role to play in preventing the risks of housing exclusion and repeat homelessness.

The ability to sustain a tenancy or maintain an independent lifestyle is more difficult at some points in the life course and is compromised by life crises (sudden loss of income, relationship breakdown, ill health and so on) or by life circumstances (learning disability or physical disability, mental ill health or drug dependency). Prevention of housing exclusion in these situations requires the provision of appropriate support for the necessary length of time required to develop the capacity of the individual to maintain independence (for some this may be permanently).

Why does homelessness and housing exclusion persist?

Earlier chapters of this volume have examined the market (Three), state (Four), and civil society (Five) mechanisms that are associated with housing exclusion and the prevention of the worst form of that exclusion – street homelessness. Structural, institutional and agency factors have been explored in this analysis. The processes by which vulnerability in the housing market is created and which can leave many low-income and vulnerable households at risk of homelessness are endemic to European capitalism, in which the economic competitiveness of the market is mediated by the redistributive actions of the state and the reciprocity of civil society. The operation of the market will continually create and recreate the conditions of vulnerability, and continuous action is required by the state to protect the most vulnerable and to provide mechanisms of redistribution which operate to ensure social stability and promote social cohesion. Despite this, it is common for policy statements to suggest that the aim of policy is to 'solve' homelessness within a defined period (see Ireland, Scotland and Finland). At the most basic interpretation it is a laudable aim of policy to aim to eradicate rough sleeping/street homelessness. However, even this is to misunderstand the process by which housing vulnerability occurs, and the dynamic factors which place households at risk in the housing market. While the Finnish policies of the 1980s had some success in reducing street homelessness, the overall level of homelessness grew and stabilised following the housing market crisis of the early 1990s. The UK government suggests that street homelessness has been reduced by two thirds since 1998. However, the number of homeless acceptances by local authorities has continued to increase in both Scotland and England, while the number of families in temporary accommodation has also increased.

This analysis suggests that structural factors create the conditions within which vulnerability to homelessness is perpetuated and in which agency factors interact to determine the scale and nature of homelessness in different societies. State intervention ostensibly aims to ameliorate the scale of homelessness or the condition of the homeless situation. In the face of the persistence of homelessness and the re-emergence of the link between poverty and inadequate and insecure housing, it is appropriate to consider why policy has had such little impact in the past.

Evidence accumulated in this volume and elsewhere indicates that, in many countries, statutory responsibility for ensuring the access of vulnerable people to adequate housing is lacking, or, at best, confused. This is normally associated with a lack of coordination of policy action at national and local levels and a lack of integration with other relevant policy areas (social services, health and employment in particular). In a period lacking in investment in housing and a retrenchment of state activity, the lack of priority accorded to housing exclusion and homelessness has often meant that inherited structures are not appropriate to deal with the problem or have not adapted to current needs. Effective intervention with regard to both these aspects requires a degree of political leadership or an 'institutional sponsor', which have been lacking. Policies have therefore tended to be reactive rather than proactive and to focus on emergency provision and alleviation rather than prevention, until very recently, in most countries.

It has been argued in another context that in order to understand housing systems better it is important to analyse the institutional capacities of the three sectors of the market, civil society, and particularly the state, vis-à-vis housing policy and delivery (Jenkins and Smith, 2001). This perspective provides a useful framework to consider some of these reasons for the limited impact of existing policy in 'solving' homelessness and preventing the perpetuation of the link between poverty and insecure or inadequate housing. Jenkins and Smith (following Grindle, 1996, p 8) refer to four elements of the measurement of state capacity: political, institutional, administrative, and technical.

Political capacity refers to an acceptance of the importance and priority to be attached to the problem of homelessness and housing vulnerability. This in itself may also require some political or administrative leadership. In the past, policies for homelessness have often tended to be reactive to a crisis or emergency – homeless people dying during a severe winter in Scandinavian countries and in Ireland and earthquake victims in Greece. Entry to the EU – and EU programme funding – allowed Portugal to focus action to tackle the problem of shanty towns. Political priority may, in some cases, require or be brought about by an institutional sponsor – in the UK for example the creation of a 'homelessness Tzar' was considered necessary to unblock the lack of success in reducing rough sleeping. Similar political leadership created the impetus to action in the Finnish homelessness policy of the late 1980s. In France, on the other hand, homelessness has been identified with the policies for social inclusion and there has been a political will to mainstream policies over a longer period.

Institutional capacity refers to national laws and policies that essentially provide the 'rules of the game' for each of the three spheres regulating action in the market, state and civil society institutions. We have drawn attention to a number of countries (Ireland, Finland, the UK, Scotland, and Germany) where recent legislation has been enacted which begins to provide clarity of responsibility and develop integrated action. We have further referred to countries, such as France, where policies have been developed within the framework of a social inclusion and social justice model in which general laws and policies (the *Loi Besson* and LOCA-PASS) provide a basis for integration of action while not defining clear statutory responsibility regarding homelessness.

The administrative capacity to deal effectively with homelessness and housing exclusion requires appropriate structures of decision making. In most countries in the past, the key agencies coping with the problem of street homelessness have, at least, been civil society organisations of the voluntary sector and the church. The perspective that homelessness is a multidimensional problem requiring action on a number of fronts including housing, social services, health, employment and education implies the need for integrated and coordinated action. This requires appropriate structures and a relationship between the public and voluntary sector to facilitate multi-agency working. It also requires adequate and appropriate funding for housing and for support which recognises the long-term nature of some preventative action as well as facilitating the short-term and transitional nature of some interventions. We have identified some evidence of new structures emerging from both state and civil society spheres. Examples include the Y-foundation in Finland; social rental agencies (SRAs) in Belgium, Germany, Italy and Spain; homelessness task forces and local forums in Ireland and Scotland; and new funding arrangements for support and housing in the UK.

Effective action to prevent homelessness and to break the link between poverty and housing exclusion also requires that the agencies of the state have the technical capacity to deal with the range of actions involved. At the most basic level this requires an understanding of the dimensions of the problem. Therefore, the state requires good intelligence, systems of data monitoring and collection, and the ability to use this information to review the effectiveness of policy. Surveys of homelessness and research on the nature of the problem are evidenced in northern European countries (France, Ireland, Finland, Germany, and Scotland). In France, for example, a major census of the homeless was undertaken in 2001 to underpin strategy. There is less evidence of structures of information systems to collate information on a continuous basis. (The Dutch KLIMOP system is, perhaps, an exception.) It is significant that new approaches to developing homelessness strategies in Ireland, the UK and Finland have placed some emphasis on the need to assess the level and nature of homelessness at the local level. This should lead to the introduction of new systems of information collection and surveys in those countries.

There are indications in some countries that recent legislation and policy action is beginning to address these 'capacity' issues, reflecting a changing perception of the nature and causes of homelessness and recognition of the structural and institutional causes as well as the relationship with individual factors. However, we suggest that, while homelessness policies have addressed the individual level and have begun to address the structural factors (at least in some countries), there is little evidence of action at the community or neighbourhood level. Policies of neighbourhood renewal and economic development have recognised the importance of social capital and have begun to develop programmes to build community capacity in relation to improving the economic competitiveness of disadvantaged neighbourhoods. The same consideration has not hitherto been evident in the policy prescription for homelessness in the state sphere or, as far as we can determine from limited evidence, in the civil society sphere of action.

Our analysis of the reasons for past policy failure must also be related to the 'marketisation' of structures and changing procedures in state and civil society agencies. The context for this in relation to improving access to housing for low-income and vulnerable groups and preventing homelessness has been the widespread 'dis'-investment in housing which has occurred during the last decade or longer. This has a direct effect in reducing the availability of affordable and adequate housing and particularly of housing allocated on the basis of social mechanisms of need. This (as we have discussed in Chapters Three and Four of this volume) has been associated with a changing attitude to risk management. Financial risk management means (for landlords in both the private and public sector) developing mechanisms that tend to exclude the riskier tenants unless there are clear underwriting guarantees from the state or voluntary sector. It often also means the postponement of the achievement of home ownership until later in the life course placing greater reliance on families or the rented sector. Organisational risk management is associated with the development of performance standards in relation to rent arrears, vacancies and antisocial behaviour that combine to increase the level of evictions. Therefore, access to housing requires not simply the availability of affordable housing. It also requires policies to minimise the financial and related risks associated with maintaining a tenancy. It further requires support for households and individuals that may be perceived as a risk to the community (people with drug or alcohol addiction or mental health problems, for example).

We have argued (Chapter Three) that there is no single housing market, but rather a multitude of regional and local housing markets with distinct characteristics. It is documented also that there is a spatial concentration of homeless service provision that often concentrates on key metropolitan areas and, in federal countries, in particular regions. Therefore, policies to prevent homelessness must recognise and tackle this spatial inequality in opportunity and choice if they are to be effective. Hitherto policies and programmes have not tended to be sensitive to the specificity of these local situations.

Helping the most vulnerable gain access to housing

Our analysis of the interaction of the market, state and civil society has given some insights into the reasons for the persistence of homelessness in its widest definition and the reasons why past policies have been ineffective in reducing or solving the problems associated with it. What then does this tell us about the policy requirements for effective action?

The overall policy aim of guaranteeing access to decent and affordable housing for all requires action that is effective and sustainable. Effective action implies that it is action that is appropriate for the households concerned. Hence, good information is needed on the nature and scale of the problems. A range of provision, as well as flexible policies, are required which relate to the variety of individual need. This will necessarily involve coordination of action within government and between agencies that will involve multi-agency working and effective partnership structures. Sustainable action recognises the processes by which homelessness and housing exclusion is created and has a long-term focus aimed at prevention. This should involve not only an understanding of how to focus intervention in relation to the pathways into homelessness, but also, importantly, at the critical transition points in the individual's life course. Policy should therefore be concerned with outcomes rather than output. To be sustainable policies should, at the level of the individual, prevent repeat homelessness. At the level of the community, homelessness strategies need to be coordinated with neighbourhood renewal and economic development. At the institutional level, intervention strategies require structures which are capable of adaptation and innovation and not stifled by funding criteria and regulation. At the structural level, homelessness strategies require to be mainstreamed into major policy areas.

Consideration of the evidence from across Europe of emerging practice, innovation in policy and practice, and 'good' practice would suggest a range of factors which need to be in place to facilitate access to housing for vulnerable and homeless people. It is to be hoped that the development of National Action Plans on Social Inclusion will raise the political priority of homelessness and housing exclusion where this has not already occurred. Given the political will to act on the problem, there then needs to be the infrastructure to guide action, and a common culture and consensus among the partners involved concerning the nature of the action required.

The infrastructure for action we suggest includes the elements of regulation and provision – legislative structure to legitimate action, strategies to guide it and appropriate resources to support it. We have described the different forms of legislation and how this is changing with new legislative provisions emerging in all countries. We have seen that several countries have developed national homelessness strategies and that these have involved the development of local action plans. Action cannot operate without the adequate level of resources targeted appropriately (that is, capital and revenue funding). Several countries have increased spending on the provision of affordable social housing (Portugal, Ireland and Finland in particular). The provision of finance to support people has been less well developed in most countries and within countries is subject to local discretion and uncertain or short-term time horizons. The UK has perhaps gone furthest in assessing need for support and coordinating action across departmental boundaries to blend mainstream resources. Other countries have begun to move in the same direction including Denmark, Germany and France. The third element of infrastructure required is a range of provision in addition to affordable housing to alleviate the emergency of homelessness and allow the transition to reintegration. This will involve both new or additional provision and, importantly, the re-provisioning of older existing accommodation to adapt the accommodation to the approach of individualised and flexible support methods.

The structure for action exists in the sense that the decentralisation of responsibilities to municipalities has occurred in most countries and there is a range of service providers in operation. However, there is a need to develop these structures in some countries (for example, in Greece) and in most countries to widen provision to cover rural areas and some federal provinces or regions. The development of umbrella agencies to act as housing providers on behalf of support agencies and homeless service providers has proved helpful in Finland and Germany and hence the institutional landscape may, in some countries, be incomplete to allow effective action to be implemented. Multi-agency working appears to be in its infancy still, and while there are some local examples of good practice in this regard, multi-agency working and the strategies required to facilitate it are not in widespread use. Local government should have a role in facilitating this but we recognise that voluntary sector initiatives have occurred without such support. Procedures for lowering the threshold to access to affordable rented housing require a range of tools. The use of social rental agencies has been described as an effective way to ease access to the private rented sector. In countries where municipal housing companies and housing associations are important social landlords, the attitude to risk management requires the adoption of performance standards in relation to issues (such as allocation, arrears, antisocial and challenging behaviour) that are not in conflict with the needs of the homeless, and low-income and vulnerable households. This will involve more flexible performance standards (for example, acceptance of higher levels of rent arrears) and also enhanced housing management techniques to sustain tenancies.

Conclusion

The Treaty of Amsterdam (1997) amendments of the Maastricht Treaty introduced to EU policy a social dimension to complement the hitherto almost exclusive concern with economic issues. Following these amendments, the Lisbon European Council meeting (March 2000) emphasised the need to set targets to eradicate poverty and social exclusion by 2010, and the European Council meeting in Nice (December 2000) approved a European Social Policy Agenda which included the implementation of National Action Plans to Combat Social Exclusion (NAPs/incl). By making explicit reference to the need to establish the right of access to decent and affordable housing the objectives of these National Action Plans introduced for the first time an explicit housing dimension to European policy, albeit a dimension which was – and is – still seen as governed by the principle of subsidiarity.

Two years on, and the NAPs/incl have undergone some evaluation. On the positive side the European Commission's evaluation suggests that all the NAPs/incl have explicitly recognised that "[a]ccess to good quality and affordable accommodation is a fundamental need and right". However, it is also apparent from the report that ensuring that this need is met still "poses a significant challenge to a number of member states" and that "developing appropriate integrated responses both to prevent and address homelessness is another essential challenge for some countries" (EC, 2002, p 51).

FEANTSA's evaluation of the NAPs/incl reflects similar concerns:

> Many NAPs refer to the homeless, and attempt to address their needs and problems with varying degrees of relevance. Many countries' proposed solutions focus on improving the housing stock, increasing the housing supply,

cutting the costs of homes, and so on. But few come up with integrated solutions.... (FEANTSA, 2002, p 3)

For the moment at least the potential of the European Social Agenda and in particular the NAPs/incl in producing coherent and focused policies for tackling homelessness and housing vulnerability have not been realised. In particular, EU policy and individual national policies designed to deal with the problems of housing vulnerability – as expressed in the NAPs/incl – fail, as the analysis of this book suggests, to recognise that effective policy requires:

> ... [a] holistic, integrated approach ... which cuts across all the different levels (prevention, emergency response, integration), spheres (housing, jobs, mental, physical and psychological health etc), groups (young people, women, men, immigrants, drug and alcohol abusers etc) and their respective needs. (FEANTSA, 2002, p 3)

References

Aglietta, M. (1982) *Régulation et crises du capitalisme: L'expérience des Etats-Unis*, Paris: Calmann-Lévy.

Aldridge, R. (2000) *Access to housing for vulnerable groups: The UK national report*, Brussels: FEANTSA.

Amin, A. and Thrift, N. (1995) 'Globalisation, institutional thickness and the local economy', in P. Healy (ed) *Managing cities: The new urban crisis*, Chichester: John Wiley & Sons, pp 102-34.

Anderson, I., Kemp, P. and Quilgers, N. (1993) *Single homeless people*, London: HMSO.

Anderson, I. and Tulloch, D. (2000) *Pathways through homelessness: A review of the research evidence*, Edinburgh: Homelessness Task Force Research Series, Scottish Homes.

Anderson, M., Bechhofer, F. and Gershuny, J. (eds) (1994) *The social and political economy of the household*, Oxford: Oxford University Press.

Arrighi, G. (1986) *Custom and innovation: Long waves and stages of capitalist development*, New York, NY: Fernand Braudel Centre.

Audit Commission (1998) *Home alone: The housing aspects of community care*, London: Audit Commission.

Avramov, D. (1995) *Homelessness in the European Union: Social and legal context of housing exclusion in the 1990s*, Brussels: FEANTSA.

Bacon, P. (2000) *The housing market in Ireland: An economic evaluation of trends and prospects*, Dublin: The Stationery Office.

BAGW (Bundesarbeitsgemeinschaft Wohnunslosenhilfe) (2000) 'Wohnfähigkeit?, Störer?, Problemhaushalte? – Soziale Ausgrenzung schwervermittelbarer Wohn ungsnotfälle aus der Versorgung mit Wohnungen und Strategien zu iher Überwindung', Positionspapier der BAGW, erarbeitet vom Fachausschuss Wohen, verabschiedet vom Gesamtvorstand auf seiner Sitzung vom 23/24, *Wohunglos*, 4/00, pp 158-62.

Balchin, P. (1996) *Housing policy in Europe*, London: Routledge.

Ball, M. (2002) *The RICS European housing review 2002*, London: Royal Institute of Chartered Surveyors.

Ball, M. and Grilli, M. (1997) *Housing markets and European convergence in the EU*, London: Royal Chartered Institute of Surveyors.

Ball, M. and Harloe, M. (1998) 'Uncertainty in European housing markets', in M. Kleinman, W. Matznetter and M. Stephens (eds) *European integration and housing policy*, London: Routledge.

Begg, I. (2001) *Social exclusion and social protection in the European Union: Policy issues and proposals for the future role of the EU*, London: EXSPRO, South Bank University.

BBR Bundesamt für Bauwesen und Raumordnung (2000) Wohnraumbeschaffung durch Kooperation. Schriftenreihe Forschungen, Heft 96, Bonn, Eigenverlag.

Betton, R. (2001) *Access to housing for vulnerable groups: The French national report 2000*, Brussels: FEANTSA.

BMVBW (Bundesministerium für Verkehr, Bau-und Wohnungswesen) (2001a) *Entwurf eines Gesetzes zur Reform des Wohnungsbaurechts*, Berlin: BMVBW.

BMVBW (2001b) *Begründung zum Entwurf eines Gesetzes zur Reform des Wohnungsbaurechts*, Berlin: BMVBW.

Boal, F. (1998) 'Exclusion and inclusion: segregation and deprivation in Belfast', in S. Musterd and W. Ostendorf (eds) *Urban segregation and the welfare state*, London: Routledge, pp 94-109.

Body-Gendrot, S. and Martiniello, M. (eds) (2000) *Minorities in European cities: The dynamics of social integration and social exclusion at the neighbourhood level*, London: Macmillan.

Boheim, R. and Taylor, M.P. (2000) *My home was my castle: Evictions and repossessions in Britain*, Colchester: Institute for Social and Economic Research, University of Essex.

Boelhouwer, P. (2000) *Financing the social rented sector in Western Europe*, Delft: Delft University Press.

Bourdieu, P. (1985) 'Social space and the geneses of groups', *Theory and Society*, vol 14, no 6, pp 723-44.

Bourgeois, M. (2000) *Van kwaad naar erger? Waalse weekendverblijfsparken en wooncarrières van vaste bewoners in sociaal-ruimtelijk perspectief*, Unpublished thesis, Institute for Social and Economic Geography, Catholic University of Leuven.

Boyer, R. (1986) *La Théorie de la Régulation: Une Analyse Critique*, Paris: La Découverte.

Bruto da Costa, A. and Baptista, I. (2001) *Access to housing for vulnerable groups: The Portuguese National Report 2000*: Brussels, FEANTSA.

Bryson, J., McGuinness, M. and Ford, R.G. (2002) 'From welfare state to the shadow state? Almshouse charities and alternative modes of welfare provision', Birmingham: School of Geography and Environmental Sciences, University of Birmingham.

Burrows, R. (1998) 'Mortgage indebtedness in England: an "epidemiology"', *Housing Studies*, vol 23, no 1, pp 5-12.

Busch-Geertsema, V. (2001) *Access to housing for vulnerable groups: The German National Report 2000*, Brussels: FEANTSA.

Carayol, R. (2002) 'A Choisy, le Bidonville de la Misère Rom', *Libération*, 20 April.

Carbrera, P. (2001) *Access to housing for vulnerable groups: The Spanish National Report 2000*, Brussels: FEANTSA.

Chapman, M. and Murie, A. (1996) 'Housing and the European Union', *Housing Studies*, vol 11, no 2, pp 307-18.

CHORE (Centre on Housing Rights and Evictions) (2000) 'Women and housing right', *Sources* 5, Geneva: CHORE.

Clarke, W.A.V. and Onaka, J.L. (1983) 'Life-cycle and housing adjustment as explanations of residential mobility', *Urban Studies*, vol 20, pp 47-57.

Committee of the Regions (1999) 'Housing and the homeless', Opinion of the Committee of the Regions, Brussels.

CNEL (1997) *Gli strumenti per una nuova politica del Comparto delle Abitazioni in Locazione*, Rome: CNEL.

Coppo, M. (1998) *Il Comparto delle Abitazioni in Locazione nelle politiche abitative locali e nazionali*, Rome: CNEL.

Corden, A. and Duffy, K. (1998) 'Human dignity and social exclusion', in R. Sykes and P. Alcock (eds) *Developments in European policy: Convergence and diversity*, Bristol: The Policy Press, pp 95-124.

Council of Europe (1996) *European Social Charter* (revised), Strasbourg: Council of Europe.

CML (Council of Mortgage Lenders) (1997) *Statistics on mortgage arrears and repossessions*, Press Release, January, quoted in J. Ford and R. Burrows (1999) 'The costs of unsustainable home ownership in Britain', *Journal of Social Policy*, vol 28, no 2, p 310.

CML (2000) *Home ownership, house purchases and mortgages: International comparisons*, London: Council of Mortgage Lenders.

Crow, G. (1989) 'The use of the concept of "strategy" in recent sociological literature', *Sociology*, vol 23, pp 1-24.

Daly, M. (1999) 'Regimes of social policy in Europe and the patterning of homelessness', in D. Avramov (ed) *Coping with homelessness: Issues to be tackled and best practices in Europe*, Aldershot: Ashgate, pp 309-30.

Davis, M. (1992) *City of quartz: Excavating Los Angeles*, London: Verso.

De Decker, P. (1994) 'Onzichtbare Muren', *Planologisch Nieuws*, vol 14, no 4, pp 341-66.

De Decker, P. (2000) *Who benefits from public money for housing in Flanders (Belgium)?*, Paper presented to the *ENHR 2000* conference in Gälve (SV), 26-30 June.

De Decker P. (2001) *Access to housing for vulnerable groups: The Belgian National Report 2000*, Brussels: FEANTSA.

De Decker P. (2002a) 'On the genesis of social rental agencies in Belgium', *Urban Studies*, vol 39, no 2, pp 297-326.

De Decker, P. (2002b) 'Op weg naar een duurzaam woonbeleid. Hoe tegenwoordig blijft het verleden? Wonen en Woomomgeving', *Welzijnsgids*, vol 44, pp 23-54.

De Decker, P. and Meert, H. (2000a) 'Dit is geen magie! Over de huisvestingsval, een onzichtbare hand en slecht besteed overheidsgeld', *Ruimte en Planning*, vol 20, no 1, pp 3-7.

De Decker, P. and Meert, H. (2000b) 'Mytisch of magisch? Over de gebiedsgerichte aanpak van sociale uitsluiting', in J. Vranken, D. Geldof and G. van Menxel (eds) *Armoede en Sociale Uitsluiting, Jaarboek 2000*, Leuven and Amersfoort: Acco, pp 59-85.

De Feijter, H. (2001) *Access to housing for vulnerable groups: The Netherlands National Report 2000*, Brussels: FEANTSA.

Dewilde, C. and De Keulenaer, F. (2002: forthcoming) 'Huisvesting: de "vergeten" dimensie van armoede', *Ruimte en Planning*, vol 22, no 2.

Dillane, J., Hill, M., Bannister, J. and Scott, S. (2001) *Evaluation of the Dundee Families Project*, Edinburgh: The Stationery Office, Scottish Executive.

Donnelly, J. (1993) *International human rights*, New York, NY: West View Press.

Donzelot, J. (ed) (1991) *Face à l'Exclusion: La Modèle Français*, Paris: Editions Esprit.

Donzelot, J. and Jaillet, M.C. (1997) *Deprived urban areas: Summary report of the pilot study*, Report no 215, Geneva: NATO.

Drummond, I., Campbell, H., Lawrence, G. and Symes, D. (2000) 'Contingent or structural crisis in British agriculture', *Sociologia Ruralis*, vol 40, no 1, pp 111-27.

Duffy, K. (1999) 'Free markets, poverty and social exclusion', in D. Avromov (ed) *Coping with homelessness: Problems to be tackled and best practices*, Aldershot: Ashgate, pp 103-26.

Durkheim E (1984) *The division of labour in society* (translated by W.D. Halls) Basingstoke: Macmillan.

Dworkin, R. (1977) *Taking rights seriously*, London: Duckworth & Co.

Economic Policy Group (nd) *Sewing up the pieces: Local authority strategies for the clothing industry*, London: LSPU.

Edgar, W. (2002) 'Housing homeless people: the Housing Association role', *Housing Today*, September 3rd.

Edgar, W. and Doherty, J. (2001) *Women and homelessness in Europe*, Bristol: The Policy Press.

Edgar, W. and Mina-Coull, A. (1998) *Supported accommodation: The appropriate use of tenancy agreements*, Edinburgh: Scottish Homes.

Edgar, W., Doherty, J. and Mina-Coull, A. (1999) *Services for homeless people: Innovation and change in the European Union*, Bristol: The Policy Press.

Edgar, W., Doherty, J. and Mina-Coull, A. (2000) *Support and housing in Europe: Tackling social exclusion in the European Union*, Bristol: The Policy Press.

Eichner, V. (1998) 'Zur Entwicklung von Sozialstruktur und räumlicher Segregation – Ist das Ende einer sozial ausgleichenden Wohnungspolitik gekommen?', in H. Brühl and C. Echter (eds) *Entmischung im Bestand an Sozialwohnungen. Dokumentation eines Seminars*, Berlin: Deutsches Institut für Urbanistik, pp 19-48.

Esping-Andersen, G. (1990) *The three worlds of welfare capitalism*, Cambridge: Polity.

Esping-Andersen, G. (1999) *Social foundations of post-industrial economies*, Oxford: Oxford University Press.

EU Working Group (2000) 'Implementing the Habitat agenda: the European Union experience', Stockholm Swedish Ministry of Foreign Affairs.

EC (European Commission) (1996) *First report on economic and social cohesion*, Luxembourg: EC.

EC (2000) *Building an inclusive Europe*, COM(200/79), Brussels: EC.

EC (2001) *Joint report on social inclusion*, Luxembourg: EC.

EC (2002) 'Draft joint report on social inclusion', Communication from the Commission to the Council, the European Parliament, the Economic and Social Committee and the Committee of the Regions, Brussels.

Falk, I. and Kilpatrick, S. (2000) 'What is social capital? A study of interaction in a rural community', *Sociologia Ruralis*, vol 40, no 1, pp 87-110.

FEANTSA (1996) 'Housing as a human right', Newsletter no 6, p 3.

FEANTSA (2001) *Promoting social inclusion through access to housing: Presentation to the 13th European meeting of Housing Ministers*, Brussels: FEANTSA.

FEANTSA (2002) 'Analysis of the national action plans – social inclusion', Brussels: (www.feantsa.org/).

Fondation Roi Baudouin (1999) *L'habitat Prolongé en Camping et en Parc Résidentiel en Region Wallone: Inventaire Descriptif – Synthèse*, Brussels: Fondation Roi Baudouin.

Ford, J. and Burrows, R. (1999) 'The costs of unsustainable home ownership in Britain', *Journal of Social Policy*, vol 28, no 2, pp 305-30, April.

Forrest, R. (2000) 'What constitutes a "balanced" community?', in I. Anderson and D. Sim (eds) *Social exclusion and housing: Context and challenges*, Coventry: Chartered Institute of Housing, pp 207-19.

Foucault, M. (1979) *The history of sexuality*, London: Allen Lane.

Franke, J. (1998) 'Permanent Wonen op Recreatieparken: Gedoogbeleid voor Chique Resorts en Rafelranden?', *Tijdschrift voor de Volkshuisvesting*, vol 4, no 2, pp 19-21.

Friedrichs, J. (1998) 'Social inequality, segregation and urban conflict: the case of Hamburg', in S. Musterd and W. Ostendorf (eds) *Urban segregation and the welfare states*, London: Routledge, pp 168-90.

Fukayama, F. (1999) *The great disruption: Human nature and the reconstruction of social order*, London: Profile Books.

GDW (Bundesverband deutshcer Wohnungsunternehmen) (1998) *Überforderte Nachbarsschaften. Zwei sozialwissenschaftliche Studien über Wohnquartiere in den alten un den neuen Bundesländern im Auftrag des GdW*, Cologne and Berlin: GDW.

Gibb, K. (2002) 'Trends and change in social housing finance and provision within the European Union', *Housing Studies*, vol 17, no 2, pp 325-36.

Giddens, A. (1979) *Central problems in social theory: Action, structure and contradiction in social analysis*, London: Macmillan.

Giddens, A. (1984) *The constitution of society: Outline of the theory of structuration*, Cambridge: Polity.

Gill, F. (2001) *Temporary accommodation for homeless people: The implications for local authorities and housing associations*, Edinburgh: Shelter Scotland.

Glennerster, H., Lupton, R., Noden, P. and Power, A. (1999) *Poverty, social exclusion and neighbourhood: Studying the area bases of social exclusion*, London: London School of Economics and Political Science.

Glomm, G. and John, A. (2001) 'Homelessness and labour markets', *Regional Science and Urban Economics*, vol 32, no 5, pp 591-606.

Goodin, R., Headey, B., Muffels, R. and Dirven, H.J. (1999) *The real worlds of welfare capitalism*, Cambridge: Cambridge University Press.

Grindle, M.S. (1996) *Challenging the state: crisis and innovation in Latin America and Africa*, Cambridge, Cambridge University Press.

Haffner, M. and van der Heijden, H. (2000) 'Housing expenditure and housing policy in the West European rental sector', *Journal of Housing and the Built Environment*, vol 15, no 1, pp 71-92.

Hall, P. (1997) 'Regeneration policies for peripheral housing estates: inward and outward looking approaches', *Urban Studies*, vol 34, nos 5-6, pp 873-90.

Hannan, C. (2000) *Beyond networks: Social cohesion and unemployment exit routes*, Colchester: Institute for Labour Research, University of Essex.

Hardy, D. and Ward, C. (1984) *Arcadia for all: The legacy of a makeshift landscape*, London: Mansell.

Harloe, M. (1995) *The people's home? Social rented housing in Europe and America: Studies in urban and social change*, Oxford: Blackwell.

Harvey, B. (1993) 'Homelessness in Europe – national housing policies and legal rights', *Scandinavian Housing and Planning Research*, vol 10, pp 115-19.

Harvey, D. (1973) *Social justice and the city*, London: Arnold.

Harvey, D. (1989) *The condition of postmodernity: An enquiry into the origins of cultural change*, Oxford: Blackwell.

Hemström, E. (2000) 'Från sluten institution, via egen bostad till hemlöshet? Om den boendessociala situationen för psykiskt störda', *PM/förstudie till den boendesociala beredningen*, January.

Henning, C. and Lieberg, M. (1996) 'Strong ties or weak ties? Neighbourhood networks in a new perspective', *Scandinavian Housing and Planning Research*, vol 13, pp 3-26.

Hillmann, F. (1999) 'A look at the "hidden side": Turkish women in Berlin's ethnic labour market', *International Journal of Urban and Regional Research*, vol 23, no 2, pp 267-82.

Holt-Jensen, A. (2000) 'Evaluating housing and neighbourhood initiatives to improve the quality of life in deprived urban areas', Paper presented at ENHR Conference, Gavle, Sweden.

Hubert, F. and Tomann, H. (1991) *Der Erwerb von Belegungsrechten im Wohnungsbestand. Eine ökonomische Wirkungsanalyse. Gutachten im Auftrage des Bundesministeriums für Raumordnung. Bauwesen und Städtebau*, Berlin.

Hütter, H. (2001) *Aufhebung des Gemeinnützigkeitsstatus der GSWB*, Presseaussendung, Salzburg, March.

Imrie, R. and Raco, M. (1999) 'How new is the new local governance? Lessons from the United Kingdom', *Transactions of the Institute of British Geographers*, vol 24, no 1, pp 45-63.

Jenkins, P. and Smith, H. (2001) 'An institutional approach to analysis of state capacity in housing systems in the developing world: case studies in South Africa and Costa Rica', *Housing Studies*, vol 16, no 4, pp 485-508.

Jessop, B. (1994) 'Post-Fordism and the state', in A. Amin (ed) *Post-Fordism: A reader*, Oxford: Blackwell, pp 251-79.

Jordan, B. (1996) *A theory of poverty and social exclusion*, Cambridge: Polity Press.

Jupp, B. (1999) *Living together: Community life on mixed tenure estates*, London: Demos.

Kärkkäinen, S. (2001) *Access to housing for vulnerable groups: The Finnish National Report*, Brussels: FEANTSA.

Kearns, A. and Forrest, R. (2000) 'Social cohesion and multi-level urban governance', *Urban Studies,* vol 37, nos 5-6, pp 995-1017.

Kemeny, J. (1995) *From public housing to the social market: Rental policy strategies in comparative perspective*, London: Routledge.

Kemp, P. (1990) 'Income related assistance with housing costs: a cross-national comparison', *Urban Studies*, vol 27, no 6, pp 795-908.

Kemp, P., Lynch, E. and MacKay, D. (2001) *Structural trends and homelessness: A quantitative analysis*, Scottish Executive, Edinburgh.

Kennedy, C., Lynch, E. and Goodlad, R. (2001) *Good practice in joint/multi-agency working on homelessness*, Edinburgh: Scottish Executive Central Research Unit.

Kesteloot, C. (2002) *Verstedelijking in Vlaanderen: Problemen, kansen en uitdagingen voor het beleid in de 21e eeuw. Task Force stedelijk beleid: Theoretisch kader*, Brussels: Ministry of the Flemish Community.

Kesteloot, C., Vandenbroecke, H. and Martens, A. (1998) 'Integratie met vallen en opstaan: over de woonsituatie van etnische minderheden in Vlaanderen', in P. de Decker (ed), *Wonen onderzocht 1995-1999*, Ministerie van de Vlaamse Gemeenschap, pp 129-55.

Kesteloot, C. and Meert, H. (1999) 'Informal spaces: the socio-economic functions and spatial location of urban informal economic activities', *International Journal of Urban and Regional Research*, vol 23, no 2, pp 233-52.

King, P. (2001) 'Conceptualising housing rights', Paper presented to HSA conference, Cardiff, September.

Kleinman, M. (1996) *Housing welfare and the state in Europe*, Cheltenham: Edward Elgar.

Kleinman, M. (1998) 'Western European housing policies: convergence or collapse', in M. Kleinman, W. Matznetter and M. Stephens (eds) *European integration and housing policy*, London: Routledge, pp 98-121.

Kleinman, M. (2002) 'The future of European Union social policy and its implications for housing', *Urban Studies*, vol 39, no 2, pp 341-52.

Kleinman, M., Matznetter, W. and Stephens, M. (eds) (1998) *European integration and housing policy*, London: Routledge.

Kleinman, M., Whitehead, C. and Scanlon, K. (1996) *The private rented sector*, London: National Housing Federation.

Koev, E. (2002) 'Finland', in M. Ball (ed) *European Housing Review 2002*, London: RICS.

Laukkanen, T. (1998) *Sosiaalisen vuokra-asumisen asukasvalinta ja valintojen valvonta 1996-1997*, Soumen ympäristö 222, Asuminen, Ympäristöministeriö, Helsinki.

Leibfried, S. and Pierson, P. (eds) (1995) European social policy: Between fragmentation and integration, Washington DC: Bookings Institution.

Lesthaeghe, R. (1995) 'The second demographic transition in western countries: an interpretation', in K. Oppenheim-Mason and A.M. Jensen (eds) *Gender and family change in industrialising countries*, Oxford: Oxford University Press, pp 17-62.

MacGregor, A. and McConnachie, M. (1995) 'Social exclusion, urban regeneration and economic reintegration', *Urban Studies*, vol 32, no 10, pp 1587-600.

Machado, M (1997) *IORU – Intervenção Operacional Renovação Urbana: Instrumento de reforço da Coesão Social*, Lisbon: Editora Vulgata.

MacIntyre, A. (1985) *On virtue*, London: Duckworth & Co.

MacLennan, D., Stephens, M. and Kemp, P. (1996) 'Housing policy in the EU member states', Report to the European Parliament, Brussels, PE166-328.

MacLennan, D. and Williams, P. (1990) 'Affordable housing in Britain and America', *Joseph Rowntree Foundation Housing Finance Series*, York: Joseph Rowntree Foundation.

Madanipour, A. (1998) 'Social exclusion and space', in A. Madanipour, G. Cars and J. Allen (eds) *Social exclusion in European cities: Processes experiences and responses*, London: Jessica Kingsley.

Maloutas, T. (1990) *Athens, housing, family: Analysis of the post-war housing practice*, Athens: Exantas (in Greek).

Malpass, P. and Murie, A. (1997) *Housing policy and practice*, Basingstoke: Macmillan.

Mayes, D., Berghman, J. and Salais, R. (2001) *Social exclusion and European policy*, Cheltenham: Edward Elgar.

Mazower, M. (2002) 'The strange triumph of human rights', *New Statesman*, 4 February, pp 15-18.

Meert, H. (1998) *De geografie van het overleven: Bestaansonzekere huishoudens en hun strategieën in een stedelijke en rurale context*, Unpublished thesis, Institute for Social and Economic Geography, Leuven: Catholic University of Leuven.

Meert, H. (2000) 'Arcadië Onderuit? Woonzones met recreatief karakter als etalageruimte voor de witte producten van de Vlaamse woningmarkt', *Ruimte en Planning*, vol 20, no 1, pp 36-50.

Meert, H. (2001) 'Space and the reproduction of residual housing outside cities: the case of inhabited campsites in Flanders', *Belgeo*, vol 2, no 3, pp 277-93.

Meert, H. (2002) 'Reciprocity, social exclusion and the regulation of the post-productivist countryside', Paper presented at the seminar *The European countryside and changing social networks*, 27 July, Brussels: Catholic University of Leuven.

Meert, H. and Bourgeois, M. (2002: forthcoming) 'Terug van weggeweest: de Parijse bidonvilles', *Ruimte en Planning*, vol 22, no 2.

Meert, H., De Rijck, T. and Bourgeois, M. (2002) *Omvang en ruimtelijk-economische dimensie van het grijze wooncircuit in Vlaanderen: een experimenteel onderzoek naar methodiekbepaling*, Brussels: Ministry of the Flemish Community.

Meert, H., Mistiaen, P. and Kesteloot, C. (1997) 'The geography of survival: household strategies in urban settings', *Tijdschrift voor Sociale en Economische Geografie*, vol 88, no 2, pp 169-81.

Meert, H., Blommaert, K., Dewilde, A., Stuyck, K. and Peleman, K. (2002) *Sociaal-geografische en discursieve analyse van attitudes van de bevolking tegenover asielzoekers*, Brussels: Federal Office for Scientific, Technical and Cultural Affairs.

Mens en Ruimte (1997): *Onderzoek naar de permanente bewoning op campings in Vlaanderen*, Brussels: Ministry of Flemish Housing.

Mingione, E. (1991) *Fragmented societies: A sociology of economic life beyond the market paradigm*, Oxford: Basil Blackwell.

Ministry of the Environment (2001) *Programme for reducing homelessness*, Helsinki: Ministry of the Environment.

Morais, I.A. (ed) (1997) *Caracterização do Programa Especial de Realojamento na Área Metropolitana de Lisboa*, Lisbon: Área Metropolitana de Lisboa – Junta Metropolitana.

Morgan, D.H.J. (1989) 'Strategies and sociologists: a comment on crow', *Sociology*, vol 23, pp 25-9.

Morokvasic, M. (1987) 'Immigrants in the Parisian garment industry', *Work, Employment and Society*, vol 1, no 4, pp 441-62.

Mouylaert, F., Swyngedouw, E. and Wilson, P. (1988) 'Spatial responses to Fordist and post-Fordist accumulation and regulation', Papers of the *Regional Science Association*, vol 64, pp 11-23.

Murie, A. (1998) 'Segregation, exclusion and housing in the divided city', in S. Musterd and W. Ostendorf (eds) *Urban segregation and the welfare state*, London: Routledge, pp 110-25.

Musterd, S. and Ostendorf, W. (1998) *Urban segregation and the welfare state: Inequality and exclusion in Western cities*, London: Routledge.

Musterd, S. and de Winter, M. (1998) 'Conditions for spatial segregation: some European perspectives', *International Journal of Urban and Regional Research*, vol. 22, no 4, pp 665-73.

Nordgaard, T. and Koch-Nielsen, I. (2001) *Access to housing for vulnerable groups: The Danish National Report*, Brussels, FEANTSA.

National Board of Housing Building and Planning (2000) *Bostadsmarknadsläge och förväntat bostadsbyggande år 2000-2001*, Boverket: Karlskrona.

Nussbaum, M.C. (2000) *Women and human development: The capabilities approach*, Cambridge: Cambridge University Press.

O'Flaherty, B. (1996) *Making room: The economics of homelessness*, Cambridge, MA: Harvard University Press.

O'Neill, O. (1996) *Towards justice and virtue: A constructive account of practical reasoning*, Cambridge: Cambridge University Press.

O'Sullivan, E. (2001) *Access to housing for vulnerable groups: The Irish National Report 2000*, Brussels: FEANTSA.

Obsourne, S.P. (1998) 'The innovative capacity of voluntary organisations: managerial challenges for local government', *Local Government Studies*, vol 21, no 1, pp 19-40.

Oxley, M. (1995) 'Private and social rented housing in Europe: distinctions, comparisons and resource allocation', *Scandinavian Journal of Housing and Planning Research*, vol 12, no 2, pp 59-72.

Oxley, M. and Smith, J. (1996) *Housing policy and rented housing in Europe*, London: E&FN Spon.

Pahl, R.E. (1984) *Division of labour*, Oxford: Basil Blackwell.

Paniagua, J.L. (1995) 'Balance y perspectives de la politica de vivenda en Espana', in L. Cortés Alcalá (ed) *Pensar la vivienda*, Madrid: Talasa, pp 45-69.

Paugam, S. (1998) 'Poverty and social exclusion: a sociological view', in M. Rhodes and Y. Mény (eds) *The future of European welfare: A new social contract*, London: Macmillan, pp 30-43.

Pawson, H. (2000) *A profile of homelessness in Scotland*, Scottish Homes, Edinburgh.

Pawson, H. and Third, H. (1997) *Review of general needs CORE log 1997*, Report to The Housing Corporation, Edinburgh: School of Planning and Housing, University of Edinburgh.

Pels, M. (2001) *Access to housing for vulnerable groups: The Luxembourg National Report*, Brussels: FEANTSA.

Péraldi, M. (2000) 'Migrants' careers and commercial expertise in Marseilles', in S. Body-Gendrot and M. Martiniello (eds) *Minorities in European cities: The dynamics of social integration and social exclusion at the neighbourhood level*, London: Macmillan, pp 44-53.

Pinder, D. (1998) *The new Europe: Economy, society and environment*, Chichester: John Wiley & Sons.

Polanyi, K. (1944) *The great transformation*, Boston, MA: Beacon Press.

Portes, A. and Landeholt, P. (1996) 'The downside of social capital', *American Prospect*, Spring, pp 35-42.

Priemus H., Kleinman M., MacLennan, D. and Turner, B. (1993) *European monetary, economic and political union: consequences for national housing policies'*, *Housing and Urban Policy Studies 6*, Delft: Delft University Press.

Priemus, H. and Boelhouwer, P. (1999) 'Social housing finance in Europe: trends and opportunities', *Urban Studies*, vol 36, no 4, pp 633-45.

Priemus, H. and Dieleman, F. (1999) 'Social housing finance in the European Union: developments and prospects', *Urban Studies*, vol 36, no 4, pp 623-33.

Pryke, M. and Whitehead, C. (1995) *Private finance and the risks of social housing provision*, Discussion Paper no 46, Cambridge: Department of Land Economy, University of Cambridge.

Putnam R. (2000) *Bowling alone: the collapse and revival of American community*, New York, NY: Simon & Schuster.

Quassoli, F. (1999) 'Migrants in the Italian underground economy', *International Journal of Urban and Regional Research*, vol 23, no 2, pp 212-31.

Rawls, J. (1971) *A theory of justice*, Oxford: Oxford University Press.

Rees, G. and Fielder, S. (1992) 'The services economy, subcontracting and the new employment relations: contract gathering and cleaning', *Work, Employment and Society*, vol 6, no 3, pp 347-68.

Rhodes, R.A.W. (1994) 'The hollowing out of the state: the changing nature of public service in Britain', *The Political Quarterly*, vol 64, pp 138-51.

Room, G. (ed) (1995) *Beyond the threshold: The measurement and analysis of social exclusion*, Bristol: The Policy Press.

Room, G. (1999) 'Social exclusion, solidarity and the challenge of globalisation', *International Journal of Social Welfare*, vol 8, pp 166-74.

Rossi, P. (1955) *Why families move*, New York, NY: Glencoe Press.

Rowntree, S. (1901) *Poverty: A study of town life*, London: Macmillan (reissued by The Policy Press in 2001).

Sabel, C.F. (1989) 'Flexible specialisation and the re-emergence of regional economies', in P.Q Hirst and J. Zeitlin (eds) *Reversing industrial decline? Industrial structure and policy in Britain and her competitors*, Oxford: Berg, pp 17-70.

Sahlin, I. (1999) *Support and housing in Sweden: National Report 1998*, Brussels: FEANTSA.

Sahlin, I. (2001) *Access to housing for vulnerable groups: The Swedish National Report 2000*, Brussels: FEANTSA.

Sainsbury, D. (1996) *Gender and welfare state regimes*, Oxford: Oxford University Press.

Samers, M. and Woods, R. (1998) 'Socio-economic change, EU policy and social disadvantage', in D. Pinder (ed) *The new Europe: Economy, society and environment*, Chichester: John Wiley & Sons, pp 241-62.

Sapounakis, A. (2001) *Access to housing for vulnerable groups: The Greek National Report 2000*, Brussels, FEANTSA.

Sarkassian, W. (1976) 'The idea of social mix in town planning: a historical review', *Urban Studies*, vol 13, pp 231-46.

Sassen, S. (1991) *The global city: New York, London and Tokyo*, Princeton, NJ: Princeton University Press.

Sayad, A. (1995) *Un nanterre Algérien, terre de Bidonvilles*, Paris: Editions Autrement.

Schoibl, H. (2001) *Access to housing for vulnerable groups: The Austrian National Report 2000*, Brussels: FEANTSA.

Scottish Executive (2001) *Helping homeless people: An action plan for prevention and effective response*, Edinburgh: Scottish Executive.

Sen, A. (1992) *Inequality re-examined*, Oxford: Clarendon Press.

Sen, A. (1999) *Development as freedom*, Oxford, Oxford University Press.

Sen, A. (2001) 'Social exclusion: concept, application and scrutiny', Social Development Papers No 1, Office of Environment and Social Development, Asian Development Bank, Manila.

Silver, H. (1994) 'Social exclusion and social solidarity: three paradigms', *International Labour Review*, vol 133, no 56, pp 531-78.

Skifter-Andersen, H. (1999) 'Housing rehabilitation and urban renewal in Europe: a cross-national analysis of problems and policies' in H. Skifter-Andersen and P. Leather (eds) *Housing renewal in Europe*, Bristol: The Policy Press.

Skifter-Andersen, H. (2000) *Sores in the face of the city: On the interactions between segregation, urban decay and deprived neighbourhoods*, Hørsholm: Danish Building and Urban Research Institute.

Somerville, P. (1998) 'Explanations of social exclusion: where does housing fit in?', *Housing Studies*, vol 13, no 6, pp 761-79.

Somerville, P. and Chan, C.K. (2002) 'Human dignity and the "third way": the case of housing policy', Paper presented at the Housing Studies Association Conference, Cardiff, September.

Sørensen, P. (1993) *Drømmenes Port, Undersøgelse af usædvanlige boligmråder*, Stockholm: SUS.

Sunia, R. (1999) *Abitazioni e famiglie in affitto: Indagine sul mercato immobiliare nazionale*, Rimini: Maggioli.

Svendsen, L.H. and Svendsen, G.T. (2000) 'Measuring social capital: the Danish Co-operative Dairy Movement', *Sociologia Ruralis*, vol 40, no 1, pp 72-86.

Taylo,r P. (1979) 'Difficult to let, difficult to live in and sometimes difficult to get out of: an essay on the provision of council housing with special reference to Killingworth', *Environment and Planning A*, vol 11 pp 1305-20.

Taylor-Gooby, P. (ed) (2000) *Welfare states under pressure*, London: Sage Publications.

Teixeira, A., Moura, D., Guerra, I., Freitas, M.J., Gros, M. and Vieira, P. (1997) *Diagnóstico de implementação fo programa PER nos municipios das areas metropolitanas de Lisboa e Porto*, Lisbon: CET/ISCTE.

The Economist (2002) 'Going through the roof', Special Report on House Prices. March 30th, Vol 364, no 8,282, pp 77-9.

Toffler, A. (1980) *The third wave*, London: Collins.

Tönnies F (1955) *Community and association* (Gemeinschaft and Gesselschaft/ translated by Charles P Loomis), London: Routledge/Kegan Paul.

Tosi, A. (1999) 'Homelessness and the housing factor: learning from the debate on homelessness and poverty', in D. Avramov (ed) *Coping with homelessness: Issues to be tackled and best practices in Europe*, Aldershot: Ashgate.

Tosi, A. (2001) *Access to housing for vulnerable groups: The Italian national report*, Brussels: FEANTSA.

Tosics, I. and Erdösi, S. (2002) 'Access to housing for disadvantaged categories of persons', Report prepared for Group of Specialists on Access to Housing, Strasbourg: Council of Europe.

Turner, B. (2000) 'Hemlöshet och bostadspolitik för alla', in W. Runquist and H. Swärd (eds) *Hemlöshet. Om oliki perspektiv och förklaringsmodeller*, Stockholm: Carlsson Bokförlag.

Törgersen, U. (1987) 'Housing: the wobbly pillar under the welfare state', in B. Turner, J. Kemeny and L. Lundqvist (eds) *Between state and market: Housing in the post-industrial era*, Stockholm: Almqvist & Wicksell International, pp 116-26.

UNCHS (United Nations Centre for Human Settlement) (2001) 'Position paper on housing rights', Geneva: UNCHS.

United Nations (1948) *Universal Declaration of Human Rights*, New York, NY: United Nations.

Van der Heijden, H. and Boelhouwer, P. (1996) 'The private rental sector in Western Europe: developments since the Second World War and prospects for the future', *Housing Studies*, vol 11, no 1, pp 13-33.

Van der Heijden, H. (2002) 'Social rented housing in Western Europe: developments and expectations', *Urban Studies*, vol 39, no 2, pp 327-40.

Vestergaard, H (1998) 'Troubled Housing Estates in Denmark', in A, Madanipour, G, Cars and J, Allen (eds) *Social exclusion in European cities*, London: Jessica Kingsley.

Volovitch-Tavares, M.C. (1995) *Portugais à Champigny, le temps des baraques*, Paris: Editions Autrement.

Vranken, J. (1999) 'Different policy approaches to homelessness', in D. Avramov (ed) *Coping with homelessness: Issues to be tackled and best practices in Europe*, Aldershot: Ashgate, pp 331-55.

Waldron, J. (1993) 'Homelessness and the issue of freedom', in J. Waldron (ed) *Liberal rights: Collected papers 1981-91*, Cambridge: Cambridge University Press, pp 36-61.

Waldron, J. (2000) 'Homelessness and community', *University of Toronto Law Journal*, vol 50, pp 371-406.

Walker, D. (2002) 'Continental drift', *Guardian*, 13 June.

Wall, E., Ferrazzi, G. and Schryer, F. (1998) 'Getting the goods on social capital', *Rural Sociology*, vol 63, no 2, pp 300-22.

Waquant, L.J.D. (1998) 'Negative social capital : State breakdown and social disruption in America's urban core', *Journal of Housing and the Built Environment*, vol 33, no. 1 pp 25-40.

Warnock, M. (1992) *The uses of philosophy*, Oxford: Blackwell.

Warrington, M.J. (1995) 'Welfare pluralism or shadow state? The provision of social housing in the 1990s', *Environment and Planning A*, vol 27, no. 9, pp 1341-60.

White, P. (1998) 'Urban life and social stress', in D. Pinder (ed) *The new Europe: Economy, society and environment*, Chichester: John Wiley & Sons, pp 305-22.

White, P. (1998) 'Ideologies, social exclusion and spatial segregation in Paris', in S. Musterd and W. Ostendorf (eds) *Urban segregation and the welfare state*, London: Routledge, pp 148-67.

Wolch, J. (1989) 'The shadow state: transformations in the voluntary sector', in J. Wolch and M. Dear (eds) *The power of geography: How territory shapes social life*, Boston, MA: Unwin Hyman, pp 197-237.

Wolch, J. (1990) *The shadow state: Government and voluntary sector in transition*, New York, NY: The Foundation Centre.

Index

Page references for figures and tables are in italics; those for notes are followed by n.

G

Other titles available from
The Policy Press

Services for homeless people
Innovation and change in thwe European Union
by Bill Edgar, Joe Doherty and Amy Mina-Coull
July 1999
£14.99
ISBN 1 86134 189 X
paperback
244 pages

Support and housing in Europe
Tackling social exclusion in the European Union
by Bill Edgar, Joe Doherty and Amy Mina-Coull
September 2000
£14.99
ISBN 1 86134 275 6
paperback
240 pages

Women and homelessness in Europe
Pathways, services and experiences
Edited by Bill Edgar and Joe Doherty
September 2001
£15.99
ISBN 1 86134 351 5
paperback
296 pages

Available from Marston Book Services
PO Box 269
Abingdon
Oxon OX14 4YN
UK
Tel: +44 (0)1235 465500
Fax: +44 (0)1235 465556
Email: direct.orders@marston.co.uk